Origins of Nation Building in the Iberian Peninsula: The Case of Early Catalonia

James W. Cortada

Arbor Hills Institute Press

Origins of Nation Building in the Iberian Peninsula:
The Case of Early Catalonia
Arbor Hills Institute Press

Interior Book Design and Layout by
www.integrativeink.com

ISBN: 978-0-6151-4203-6

TABLE OF CONTENTS

CHAPTER FIVE CONSEQUENCES FOR CATALONIA: SOME CONCLUDING THOUGHTS

PREFACE

Catalonia occupies the northeastern corner of Spain, and spills over into France. It has had its own distinct language, apart from Spanish or French, for over a thousand years, and a history and culture unique to the region. How that circumstance originated is the subject of the essays in this short monograph. Much has been written about the history of Catalonia of the late Middle Ages to the present, and today it remains a subject of considerable discussion in modern Spain. Its largest city, Barcelona, has been an important economic center in the Iberian Peninsula and today is one of the most energized commercial centers in Europe.

One of the most important, thorny historical problems that Spaniards have faced for some two thousand years can be summarized in one word: regionalism. Maps show a united Spain from the Pyrenees along the French border to the Rock of Gibraltar. However, Spain more often than not has been a conglomeration of loosely knitted together regions, normally under Castilian control, but not always. Regional nationalism has often led to wars and other political and social conflagrations and most recently to the creation of a federated representative democracy nominally headed by a king. It has dogged the Spanish experience since the earliest of times. The essays in this monograph actually demonstrate that regionalist characteristics can be identified even during the prehistory of Catalonia, with the arrival of early "cave men," as people are want to call their earliest ancestors. The problem of centrifical/peripheral regionalist politics has involved the same players: Basques, Catalans, central Iberians (Castilians) in well documented ways for over a thousand years, although even then, one can argue that the problem predated even that chronology. In reading today's newspapers in Spain, with coverage of Basque issues, Catalan culture in full bloom, of international trade from Barcelona, and centralist government policies in Madrid, one is brushing very close to familiar issues from almost any century in Spanish history.

Put another way, the institutional and legal trappings of the past are alive and well. As a specific instance, there is the influence of Roman law on modern Spanish jurisprudence. One still confronts passionately local rights (*fueros*), some of which date back nearly one thousand years while most only from the latter Middle Ages. Of course, there is the monarchy's survival. That institution in its current form first emerged through the union of Ferdinand and Isabel over five hundred years ago and was partially influenced (but hardly modified significantly) by the French style of politics in the eighteenth century. The famous bond of Ferdinand and Isabel was no accident; it culminated a process of dynastic monarchical consolidations of political entities with a history of at least fifteen hundred years of war, marriages, and tribulations. Catalonia experienced all of that as it was formed first into a region and then coupled to the Spanish nation.

In the chapters ahead, which take the story of the creation and evolution of Catalonia into a region to 1035 A.D., we will see that Spain's very remote past has much to teach us about modern Iberian society. While it would be presumptuous to argue too emphatically that what happened, say, one or two thousand years ago is directly evident today, nonetheless, those familiar with Spanish society will find much which is similar in the following pages, almost as a relative of modern times. In particular, Iberians from Roman times through those living in the Middle Ages as well, left a heavy imprint on the face of Spain which is still very recognizable today. In short, it my belief that it would be difficult for historians of contemporary Spain, political scientists interested in current events, and political leaders not to learn useful lessons from that past. A look at the last one hundred to two hundred years of Spanish history, therefore, will not do the job. A look at the distant roots of modern Spanish political behavior is possible, useful, and just too important to be left to historians of the earliest periods. Inhabitants of the twenty-first century world must learn too from the past.

If this contention is so for Spaniards at large, it is even more critical for Catalans because their region is always in a contentious relationship with the rest of Spain in terms that are vital to the welfare of individual Catalans. To be sure, Catalans publish a great deal of historical literature on their region; however, one has to wonder how much of it is read because of its limited publication runs and often arcane focus. Consolidating general trends in highly approachable ways is needed. This monograph attempts to do that for one of the least understood, most fragmented parts of Catalan history, and that is often some of the most complicated historical issues for anyone to study. For those outside of Catalonia, who do not even read Catalan—the language in which so much local history has been written—it is even more of a problem to resolve.

So why end this story at 1035? It is a good stopping point because extant evidence suggests strongly that the roots of Spanish and Catalan political behavior were in place by then. After 1035 events played out leading to the creation of a Spanish nation-state with characteristics it has retained to the present. It is my contention that the roots of Catalan and Spanish political behavior were nurtured into recognizable form well over a thousand years ago and that these gave definition and perspective to modern patterns of behavior. More specifically, the roots give us a greater measure of appreciation for some of the central issues of modern Spanish politics: survivability of democracy and the nature of regionalism. I chose to examine these issues through the prism of one region, Catalonia.

The first chapter addresses the issue of who were the first humans to occupy what eventually became known as Catalonia, our "cave men." What the evidence shows is that it almost seemed as if there was as much traffic of peoples coming and going as one might observe on the Diagonal or the Ramblas in modern Barcelona. Various ethnic groups came and went and lived out their social, economic, political, and military lives in this area. There were so many peoples that one could facetiously wonder why they did not wear out the footpaths of the Pyrenees, particularly at the eastern end. The second essay focuses on the Roman experience because the effects of this period on Catalan history, particularly its architectures for centuries and its laws for over a millennium would be difficult to overstate. Language, law, municipal institutions, Castilian authoritarianism, and Catalan bewitchment with legal considerations all came out of their Roman experience. Furthermore, one can reasonably argue, although albeit difficult to measure, that attitude towards law and government emerged out of this Roman experience, including about the function of the Catholic Church which had such solid Roman foundations. When one considers that Roman sway in Catalonia and Iberia as a whole lasted some six hundred years, and which led to both becoming the most Romanized province of the entire empire, indeed not vanishing even with the Visigothic invasions, perdued by melting into an Iberian Hispano-Roman-Visigothic potpourri, made Roman roots clear and very important to all involved.

The third essay takes the story forward, threading the Roman inheritance through subsequent periods, most notably the era of Charlemagne and the whole issue of French-Catalan contacts and interactions. It is as complicated a story as that told in the first two essays. But by 1035, as a general statement for both Catalonia and most of the Iberian Peninsula, the Latin inheritance was permanently imbedded in the advancing Christian Iberian nations only to be reinforced with time as the reception of Roman law eventually spread anew throughout Western Europe.

One feature of very early Catalonia, and for that matter all Iberian history, was the role of dynastic affairs. It is evident from the facts of history that from the very beginning of recorded Iberian history, marriages were a way of conducting diplomacy and creating alliances, including in Catalonia. Expansion and consolidations were largely the product of dynastic unions, and not simply the result of the force of arms. In each chapter, I discuss in what may seem excruciating detail many such unions for that reasons. But I can assure you that the same was going in every other kingdom and region in Iberia and across all of Europe, Africa, and Asia. It was how things were done until essentially the twentieth century. In the case of Spain, the ultimate fruition of the process was, of course, the marriage of Ferdinand and Isabel, which brought together into one monarchy Castile and Aragon. In the process of this union at "the top," however, the various regions affected retained their separate legal and social characteristics, including local languages. While geography contributed undoubtedly to the maintenance of particular identities, the end result of this dynastic union was a conglomerate of several nations with loyalty to the monarch and not necessarily to the nation as such. Each region still characterized itself by its local identify, so Catalans were still citizens of Catalonia while the Basques remained Basque, and Castilian Castilians. In other words, during the Middle Ages, each region was considered as separate nationalities within the geographic region of Spain. This assessment is not too unlike a Frenchman or a German who today consider themselves European (or a member of the European Union), but nationally as belonging to the French or German nation. So, to put things bluntly, so much has not changed for the Catalans or the politicos who function in Madrid.

In the case of Catalonia, we have the specific issue of the influence of France, beginning with Charlemagne, and really extending through the nineteenth century. However, it is in the third essay that I address the initial question of the French influence on Catalan affairs, because it is in the era of Charlemagne that much happens in the formulation of Catalan identity and early politics and social behavior, and the French affect Catalan activities down to the present. Simply put, areas under Charlemagne's control had a sufficiently different experience in law, politics, diplomacy, and obviously cultural heritage from other areas, to imprint upon Catalan provinces a socio-political heritage influential on events over many subsequent centuries. These are patterns of behavior that remain familiar even today nearly a thousand years later.

Lastly, I would like to highlight the fact that from the start of the Middle Ages a contrast between the type of economies which evolved in Castile and Aragon on the one hand, and Catalonia on the other, becomes evident with political consequences, even during the earliest period of Catalan history described in this monograph. For many centuries, central Spain remained essentially agricultural and pastoral, while the Catalonian economy evolved more quickly into industry and commerce, with the development of merchant and military fleets of ships, and evolved in Catalonia with Barcelona as a major hub of international trade. One result of this macro-trend was the absence in Castile of a broad middle class, an essential requirement for the beginnings of any democracy. In Barcelona, as a concomitant of the growth of industry and commerce, a legally minded middle class developed which expanded beyond urban territories. Law and order were and remain important for the health of a commercial economy; hence Catalonia's tendency towards legal approaches which became an important factor in the Catalan psyche. In Castile, peasantry retained to a higher degree a sense of personal dignity and honor as a byproduct of feudal imperfect evolution combined with early frontier traditions. It is an important reason, when combined with the nature of trade and commerce, for why there was an absence of a middle class, the dearth which impeded development of representative government over many hundreds of years. The bottom line on Spain's political heritage is that centralistic versus regionalist, or peripheral, politics remains a clearly traceable and discernable feature of modern Spanish affairs.

The reader may reach the conclusion that the history told here is terribly elitist and old fashion, with too much attention paid to who rules when in Catalonia. But that is because of the nature of dynastic familial politics, which were so profoundly characteristic of pre-modern European societies. So, this monograph has to be a narrative of dynasties, of kings and counts hungry for power and wealth, rather than a survey of peasants and the unknown urbanites. I admit it runs against current fashion in historical circles. Partly, my thrust is a function of where available documentation took me, but also because politicos were nobles and warriors; on occasion they were strong willed ladies and priests. Given the fact that there is much confusion in the historical literature on the period, yet a growing body of up-to-date summaries on early Spanish history, I paid careful attention to sorting out who were the rulers, mover, and influencers of early Catalonia, explaining and summarizing modern research. Most research has been aimed at narrow audiences of historians, linguists, archaeologists, and cultural anthropologists. My intention was to reach an audience not expert in some particular aspect of early Catalan history and in defense of my concern about Iberia's early political heritage.

Of course, the further back in time one goes, the less available good historical evidence exists, and the more writers speculated about what really happened, and why. It was and remains a thorny problem for anyone looking at the very earliest history of Catalonia. That said, there are many contemporary chronicles one can examine and it is amazing how much ephemera has survived, particularly for the period beginning after the Roman occupation of Spain.

There is one personal issue to be addressed. If the reader is a Catalan knowledgeable about modern Catalan history, they will recognize that my name is both Catalan and famous. My family came from the province of Gerona, migrated to the New World in the 1840s, and I am thoroughly a citizen of the United States, a real Anglo. My father was born in New York, raised in Cuba, served as a U.S. diplomat for 32 years, and as Consul General in Barcelona from 1967 to 1970. We collaborated on early research on Catalan history, and the first chapter started out as an article we wrote jointly. He knew a great deal about Catalan history and was named an *académico correspondiente* in 1971 of the Real Academia de Buenas Letras of Barcelona. I earned a Ph.D. in European history with a specialty in Spanish history, and subsequently published a number of books on Spanish affairs.

Another way Catalans know the name Cortada is because during the Spanish Civil War (1936-39) there was a Roldán Cortada, who was an important labor and political leader in Barcelona who was assassinated on April 25, 1937. Two days later tens of thousands of Catalans attended his funeral and Luis Companys, the president of Catalonia, led the procession. For decades Catalans asked my father and I if we were his relatives. To the best of our knowledge, we were not. Finally, in the spirit of full disclosure, I need to mention Juan Cortada (1805-1868), a distant relative, who was a lawyer, journalist, professor, and historian best remembered for being one of the earliest promoters of what became the resurgence in Catalan nationalism in the nineteenth century, when he published a pan-Catalan pamphlet, *Cataluñu y los Catalanes* in 1860, a compilation of articles he had published in a local newspaper (*Telegrafo*) in 1859. I am not a pan-Catalanist, merely an American historian pointing out the most obvious about Catalan history.

While any errors of fact or judgment are my own fault, I want to take this opportunity to thank those Catalans and other historians who have helped me over the years. The great twentieth century Catalan book dealer, Josep Porter, introduced me to Catalan history. Professor Pedro Voltes Bou, of the University of Barcelona, imbued me with the importance of understanding thoroughly Catalan economic history, while the American Hispanist, Professor Stanley G. Payne, encouraged me to study and publish history about the Iberian Peninsula. Finally, no study of Catalan history is complete without the support of the monks of the monastery at Montserrat, who protect one of the great libraries in Europe. Please engage me in dialogue about the topics in this book. These days I can be reached at jwcorta@us.ibm.com or at 2917 Irvington Way, Madison, Wisconsin 53713, United States.

James W. Cortada

CHAPTER ONE
PREHISTORIC REGIONALISM IN THE IBERIAN PENINSULA: THE EVIDENCE FOR CATALONIA

The four provinces which occupy the northeast corner of the Iberian Peninsula, known as Catalonia (Cataluña, Catalunya), posed collectively numerous and profound historical problems for Spain. For hundreds of years this region boasted its own language, culture, legal institutions, and history, separate from those of Castile. Catalonia resisted continuously the centralist tendencies of Castilian governments and today its citizens still consider themselves Catalan as well as Spanish. During the Middle Ages the Aragonese kingdom, which was in large part itself Catalan, was a major power in the Mediterranean world while at the same time Castile was involved in its unification and reconquest of Arab lands in the peninsula. In the nineteenth and twentieth centuries regionalism became one of the fundamental political problems of Spain and the Catalans were at the center of that issue, sharing with the Basques an age-old struggle with Madrid. Thus, historians of Spanish history always have to contend with Catalonia in any century they choose to study.

Most historians will argue that Catalonia became a separate society from Castile's during the Roman occupation of the Spanish Peninsula, or in the High Middle Ages. However, it is possible to trace far earlier points of separation between the coastal north-east and central Spanish societies, even before the Greco-Roman penetration into Iberia. Therein lies the major significance of archaeological research into the area's past, an initiative that has continued to the present and for over a century in a serious and professional manner. Work in Catalan prehistory

1

suggests that Catalans were already developing differently from the inhabitants of the central regions earlier than many historians of modern Spain realized as late as the 1970s and 1980s. While many argued that Castile was populated and endowed with characteristics originating in North Africa and Middle Eastern societies, of which most has been written, little was said about Spanish Catalonia. To be sure, particularly during the Franco Regime, commenting on the virtues of some peripheral region in historical terms proved difficult, if not impossible, to get past the censors. But the focus on Castile had been a dominant theme in earlier decades of the twentieth century, a period in which highly skilled and prolific historians around the world had focused on the centrality of the Castilian experience. Archaeologists in the 1950s and 1960s flew under the radar, so to speak, of Francoist censors and thus could work with greater freedom of exploration and expression not enjoyed by Spanish scholars in general until after dictator Francisco Franco's death in 1975. Since then, there has been a remarkable renaissance in all manner of Spanish history that has restored the profession to a central position in modern historiography. But, as in most regions of Spain, there is considerable catch-up in work to do, not the least of which concerns the evolution of regional distinctions. The case of Catalonia is no exception.

Although Catalan society extends into southern France, for the purpose of this essay, my focus is on Catalonian experiences and events that took place in the Iberian Peninsula.

The story of human habitation in the Catalan region obviously begins with people coming into the area. Humans migrated into the northeast corner of Spain from across the Pyrenees, while some came possibly from other areas in the Mediterranean world. In short, the cave men of Catalonia were of European origin. Later one might speak of them as Latinized or even French in more modern times. Admittedly, the prehistory of Iberia remains a jumbled mess, despite considerable recent research, and confuses historians who wrote more often on Castilian antiquity and less on the north. A brief survey of what is known about Catalan prehistory suggests that at an early age in man's development, the Catalans were already set on a destiny different from Castile's. Moreover, this essay should serve to remind us that prehistoric societies in Iberia varied, as in the rest of Europe, making it difficult to draw broad confident conclusions for use by historians, political scientists, and economists working on modern Spain.

Scholarship on Catalonia

While prehistorians in other parts of Western Europe in the nineteenth century were rapidly discovering the complexities of prehistoric societies outside of Spain, a similar process was underway with regard to Catalonia. It only seemed reasonable to study Catalonia apart from Castile since the northern sector was affected profoundly by Europe's cultural evolution and especially by events in neighboring France. Early efforts in Catalonia centered on problems related to the origins of numerous megalithic monuments, found mostly in the upper half of Catalonia nearest France. The primary early major work on Catalan prehistory appeared in the 1870s as a consequence of such studies.[1]

The first significant work on Catalonia of lasting value was done by a Catalan, Antonio de Bofarull, who studied dolmens in the province of Barcelona. In a rather biting fashion he ridiculed those who credited Spain's primitive inhabitants as dolmenic monument builders, alleging that their lack of "civilization" made such an assumption untenable.[2] Despite his rejection of the idea that Catalan megaliths belonged to an extremely remote period, others searched for ancient remains. A leading Spanish historian of the nineteenth century, Marcelino Menéndez y Pelayo, joined with Bofarull in rejecting the notion of great Catalan antiquity. Yet a growing number of scholars subsequently challenged this position.[3]

During the first quarter of the twentieth century, interest in Catalan prehistory broadened and was marked by continuous explorations by amateurs and a growing number of professionals. Hugo Obermaier, professor at the Central University of Maddrid, and his associate Antonio García Bellido, and Pedro Bosch Gimpera of the University of Barcelona, joined with others to explore in Catalonia. Juan Cabré Aguiló, Luis Pericot García, Julio Martínez Santa-Olalla, and José Pérez de Barradas contributed their talents toward developing scientifically-verifiable knowledge of Catalonian prehistory.[4]

In the mid-twentieth century Miguel Tarradell Mateu, of the University of Valencia, summarized most of what was known about the area's past up the establishment of the Greek trading colony at Ampurias in what eventually became known as the province of Gerona.[5] The difficulty he faced in such a task grew out of the confusing evidence and sparse reliable facts available to the prehistorian. Even contemporary scholars such as Louis Pericot, Miguel Oliva, and Juan Maluquer de Motes complained of the dearth of reliable information, thus reflecting the problems faced by prehistorians in other parts of Europe.

During the last quarter of the twentieth century, considerable work was done in exploring the Catalan region by archaeologists, filling in details, gathering evidence, sharing findings through conferences, and by expanding the scientific literature on Catalonia's prehistory.[6] This initiative was part of the more global movement of scholars exploring the origins of humankind and their early civilization, leading to the emergence of a new class of historians known as world historians, and who relied extensively on these local field research projects.[7]

Pre-Neolothic Evidence

Despite these difficulties, much data has been gathered about prehistoric humankind in Catalonia for various epochs. Going into the extreme past to the early or lower Palaeolithic ages, however, no human remains have as yet been found in Spain or Portugal. Artifacts of suspected Chellean origins (300,000 to 500,000 years ago) have been located at Constantí in the Catalan province of Tarragona, at San Blas in neighboring Teruel province, and at a few miscellaneous sites in the Iberian Peninsula. On the other hand, some Neanderthal fossilized remains from the middle Paleolithic or Mousterian age were identified in widely-separated sites. Thus, in the Third Interglacial and Fourth Glaciation eras, Neanderthal man most likely roamed throughout large portions of Spain and Portugal as he did in Western Europe and in the Middle East. As far south as Gibraltar, a female skull was found in 1848 later identified as Neanderthal in origin, along with the skeleton of a roughly five-year old child discovered in the same region in the 1930s. Part of a Neanderthal jaw uncovered in Gerona province also appeared to be of similar origin.[8]

Generally, Catalan Upper Palaeolithic findings appear to reflect a strong influence derived from the French side of the Pyrenees. Furthermore, it seemed quite certain that there was no linkage on the Spanish side in that particular period between developments in the Cantabric region and that of Catalonia, neither around the Pyrenees nor southward in the central plains. On the other hand, a strong cultural link, clearly evident on the French slopes and foothills of the Pyrenees, suggested that the Upper Palaeolithic culture flanked both ends of this mountain range and entered into Spain. Thus, a community of culture existed in France and Catalonia which grew in identity, at least down to the fourth century B.C. Yet despite intensive search in Catalonia, relatively few Upper Palaeolethic sites have been found in comparison with those of France, particularly in the area around the Dordogne, and for that matter, in the Spanish Cantabric region. Luis Pericot had postulated that the population of Catalonia apparently was considerably less than the Cantabric areas.[9] As confirmation of Pericot's supposition, findings to the present time in Catalonia have little in common with the Paleolithic discoveries made in central and southern Spain.

Important sites were discovered for the Middle and Upper Palaeolothic periods in Catalonia, however, which do provide evidence of early human habitation of the area. At Cogul, in Lerida province, there is a rock-ledge painting showing nine women dancing around a male who looks somewhat like a satyr. The breasts hang, bell-shaped skirts are drawn, their legs seem robust, and some jewelry adorns the triangular-shaped heads. The male wears a type of garter. At these sites artifacts from various stages of the Upper Palaeolithic were found mixed or in layers, and not just at Cogul. Obviously, such caves and rock ledges served as shelters for successive peoples and cultures over thousands of years.[10] In Parpallo in Valencia there are rock paintings definitely belonging to the Solutrean era. Considerable differences of opinion among Spanish and foreign specialists remain regarding whether the paintings at Cogul, at other Catalan sites, and elsewhere in Spain and France could be dated to the Palaeolithic period. Some controversy also exists on whether they were the work of later artists of the Neolithic era.

The theory that the Aurignacian culture had its origins either in Africa or Asia, with currents moving into both Europe and

North America, finding common ground in Western Europe, came increasingly under attack in the late twentieth century. Some still argue that Spain's sub-stratum of population is originally of African derivation, possibly stemming from people arriving from Africa in the area of Gibraltar. Others, equally adamant in their views, maintain that at most, African influence in the Upper Palaeolithic confined itself only to a few spots in southern Spain. They insist that the Aurignacian stream moved gradually into Spain from France around the ends of the Pyrenees. In the Catalan sites, however, French-oriented Aurignacian artifacts and Gravetian finds were found together.

The question of whether or not a Mesolithic stage existed in Catalonia is still not fully resolved. Juan Maluquer de Motes, a leading Catalan prehistorian in the twentieth century, maintained that "in the present stage of our knowledge, it is not possible to decide definitively whether or not there existed a Mesolithic stage in Catalonia prior to the development of the first forms of Neolithic life."[11] Nevertheless, some indications of the Azilian culture have been found in Serinyá in Gerona province, and in a level at San Gregori near Falset in the province of Tarragona. At Cau del Duc near Torroella de Montgrí, south the of the Pyrenees and close to the Costa Brava, and at Ullá (also in Gerona province), some artifacts bear a similarity to the Asturian industry of Mesolithic vintage characteristic of certain sites in northwestern Spain and contemporary with the Azilian. Skeletal remains for the Mesolithic stage in Catalonia, however, have yet to be uncovered. Lastly, the Tardenoisian industry and the Final Capsian, also related to the Mesolithic, are both believed to be of North African inspiration, possibly entering France through Spain. Yet apparently these did not leave any remains in Catalonia. In the Iberian Peninsula the Final Capsian culture was located in the south and centre, the Tardenoisian in the north, while other Mesolithic artifacts appear in the far west in present-day Portugal.

Links to France

The Neolithic period in Spain represented a major revolution in man's cultural development, as it did in so many other parts of Europe. The gradual shift over the centuries from hunting and food gathering to settled agriculture and animal domestication led to considerable population expansion throughout Europe, including in Catalonia. This development in turn resulted in new forms of social interrelationships as primitive tribes sought ways of coping with the consequences of greater numbers. Thus, the Neolithic era can be considered as the time when the earliest roots of European, Spanish, or Catalan civilization took hold. Much of man's development at this point came about because of climatic changes rather than through some genetic evolution, as the Mediterranean basin became similar to that of today.[12]

With respect to the appearance of Neolithic culture in its earliest phases in Catalonia and in France, the geography of northeastern Spain must be considered. At the risk of being pedantic and obvious, terrain was profoundly important to the evolution of any early human society. People moved by walking; rivers drew them for water; while contours of the land afforded shelter or exposure, protection from danger. The four provinces constituting Catalonia in Spain, roughly triangular in shape, cover some 12,500 square miles. Catalonia is largely a ruggedly mountainous country with spurs extending from the Pyrenees mostly towards the Mediterranean. Other ranges spread to the southwestern section of the general area, the most important of which, the Sierra de la Llena, practically divides Catalonia in two. About twenty-six rivers originate in this watershed, none of them navigable. Some move eastward to the Mediterranean and others are tributaries of the Ebro, such as the Segre. Still others flow into the Segre. The Noguera Pallaresa and the Noguera Ribagorzana are among the tributaries of the Segre, while the Llobregat, Fluvía, Francolí, and Tordera empty directly into the Mediterranean.

Interspersed among the various mountain ranges are valleys of remarkable fertility and the plateau in upper Catalonia, almost immediately south of the Pyrenees. As the mountains near the coast, their grade slowly diminishes and wider areas are more suitable for cultivation and become available, particularly along the 240-mile coastal strip which broadens out considerably toward the Mediterranean end of the Castilian triangle. Climatic conditions changes little in Catalonia from the late Neolithic or early Bronze Age. There was probably somewhat greater rainfall than at present, judging by the greater degree of desiccation now evident in southern Spain and North Africa. While temperatures in the Catalan Pyrenees reflect characteristics typical of a temperate zone, those in the lowlands are somewhat like those in northern Florida or southern Georgia.

Despite the ruggedness of the Pyrenees, crossing into the Catalan provinces from France presented no unsurmountable problem to the Neolithic peoples, just as hikers today find the process quite manageable, indeed "fun." There are numerous passes which could easily be used by the foot traveler, and that have continued to be used over the millennia by smugglers, travelers, and even Civil War refugees in the 1930s. The Col de Perthus, for example, is rarely if ever blocked by bad weather. Massive movement of peoples might readily have taken place at the eastern end of the Pyrenees, as happened in the more modern times of recorded history. The Catalan coast does not have deep water ports other than at Barcelona and Tarragona, both of which were artificially constructed to meet modern needs. Seafarers of the middle or late Neolithic periods, however, would have found the many miles of sandy beaches and the small alcoves of the Costa Brava in what is now Gerona province, and located south of the Pyrenees, for primitive Mediterranean vessels. Toward the west, the steppe-like Monegros desert in Aragón certainly presented Neolithic inhabitants with an obstacle to travel into the interior of Spain. The natural barrier of the Ebro River valley, coupled with the mountainous character of Catalonia, confined Neolithic people to regions relatively near the coast or to the southeast of the Pyrenees. Thus, Catalonia's link with southern France has roots reaching to the dawn of Catalan and European history. The geography gave the area an identity different from that of other parts of Spain for many years.[13]

Evidence for the link to the north appeared in other forms as well. In the 1920s in a cave near the Benedictine monastery of Montserrat, close to Barcelona, archaeologists uncovered for the first time in Catalonia a primitive type of pottery characteristic of the early Neolithic period. Because this pottery was decorated with shell impression of *L. Cardium Edule*—a type of mollusk— they called it Cardium pottery. In time, other finds of similar pottery were made throughout Catalonia in caves near the coastal regions. The Catalan discoveries linked the early Neolithic culture of the region to that of southern France and northern Italy where Cardium-type pottery was found along with bone and polished stone artifacts typical of the transnational stage from Mesolithic to early Neolithic life. With minor differences this culture appeared to have diffused widely throughout the western Mediterranean coastal regions. Hatchets, adzes, gouges, chisels, hammers and other stone implements found in many Mediterranean sites confirmed the extent of this diffusion.[14]

Neolithic Societies

In Catalonia the cave culture of the early Neolithic people probably evolved, either as a result of foreign intrusion or through natural development, into a way of life away from the rocky shelters. Current thinking places the cause for the enormous transition that occurred in Neolithic societies in Europe more at the feet of changing climate than to some evolution in the physical nature of humans.[15] Judging by the location of burial sites, the evolving Neolithic culture required living in the open in lowland areas near rivers, brooks, and springs. These unsettled agriculturalists buried their dead at some depth in the open in box-shaped containers made of stone slabs sometimes referred to as Neolithic cists. In Catalonia, where over one hundred of such sites had been found just by the mid-twentieth century, material discovered includes stone tips, plain pottery, miscellaneous polished stone implements, and necklaces made of blue-green translucent beads. At one time, Spanish archaeologists felt strongly that the Catalan Neolithic pattern reflected in the stone cist culture represented an extension of the somewhat similar contemporary culture of Almeria in Andalusia in southern Spain. The vast and important discoveries at Los Millares lent weight to the contention that Almeria might have been the center of a culture which eventually reached southern France, Switzerland, and northern Italy by passing through Catalonia. A leading Catalan prehistorian, Miguel Tarradell Mateu, advanced impressive arguments against this view, although not denying that they were both contemporary cultures and part of a widespread Mediterranean phenomenon.[16]

Neolithic culture similar to the Almerian existed in northern Italy at La Logozza, in southeastern Switzerland, and in southern France. Other finds have been made of a similar type in other parts of Italy as well. In 1949-1950 Maluquer de Motes linked the pottery found at La Lagozza, that of Chassey in France, and that of Cortaillod in Switzerland, to those artifacts found in Catalan burial sites. Tarradell, however, pointed out important differences between the Catalan burial sites and findings in these tombs with those in Almeria. In addition to problems of chronology, Almeria's precluded the role of Catalonia as a bridge to Europe for an early Neolithic Almerian culture.[17]

Another stage of Neolithic life following the cist burial culture was the impressive Megalithic tomb phase, also found widespread throughout Europe in the same general period. Since specialists are becoming more convinced today that this phase did not reflect Middle Eastern influences but rather European origins, Catalonia's experience becomes more important. Ironically, more is known about Catalan Megalithic culture than on any other prehistoric stage of this region. Over two hundred Megalithic sites have been found, mostly in the northern half of Catalonia. South of the Ebro River in Valencia important Megalithic finds have also been located, and to a limited extent, southward to Almeria and Granada provinces and in the Basque country to the north. Finds in the Aragonese Pyrenees between the Basque region and Catalonia could be a tenuous cultural link for the period between the two regions. While the specific kinds of artifacts, their qualities and quantities, vary greatly in Megalithic sites, they nevertheless have in common the basic characteristics of the stone monumental burial structures found throughout Europe.

There is only speculation concerning the origins of Megalithic culture. Whether the new culture was brought into Europe from the Middle East, a theory that was long in vogue, or from some other place, or another answer is needed, is still puzzling. Regarding Catalonia, the unresolved dilemma also concerns the source of the Megalithic culture so prevalent in the upper half of the region. As early as 1925, Luis Pericot García had concluded that Catalan dolmenic culture had extended from about 2,500 B.C. to 1,000 B.C., during which time use of copper and bronze was gradually introduced by traders from the Middle East.[18] In contrast, the brilliant El Algar civilization in Almeria, not to be confused with the much earlier and probably unrelated Almerian culture of Los Millares, may have reached its apogee about 1,600 B.C.[19] There is very little evidence to support the contention that there was any close contact between the Megalithic culture phenomenon in Catalonia and the Algarian. On the other hand, developments in southern France seemed to parallel those in Catalonia, implying some connection. Increasingly, historians of the most distant past of Europe and the Middle East have pushed back the chronology when communities interacted with each other, suggesting for our purposes, that groups of people may have interacted on a regular basis on both sides of the Pyrenees, a circumstance that obviously becomes even more the case the closer to the present one looks at.

Post- Neolithic Periods

The Aeneolithic or Copper Age existed in Spain from about 2,500 B.C. to approximately 2,000 B.C., although carbon calibration has been pushing these dates backward, perhaps as much as to 4,000 B.C. It was a transition period, however, that melted imperceptibly into the more substantive Bronze Age. It overlapped many areas, including Catalonia. Of greater importance during the copper period was the Bell Beaker culture which had its origin in Spain. There have been various theories put forth on the spread of Beaker culture from Spain to the rest of Europe, but the proposals most widely accepted point to both ends of the Pyrenees as the movement's routes, rather than to sea travel. This presumes some degree of migration northward by late Neolithic people from Spain. From Catalonia it could be supposed that the Beaker carriers found their way into Provence and Languedoc in France by passing through Le Perthus to the eastern Pyrenees. Ancient Greeks and Romans, writing misty accounts of the western Mediterranean, acknowledge an early connection among tribes in southern France between the Pyrenees and the Rhône River and those in Catalonia. Current thinking suggests that beaker culture is less about new tribes and peoples than about the evolution of technologies and practices, spread by traders and other transients moving along river beds, passes, and trails.[20]

The Argaric culture (which preceded the Iron Age) became widely extended throughout Spain at the same time that bronze was also in general use in Europe. But Catalonia, poor in metals, was out of the main cultural stream during the Bronze Age, judging from the relative paucity of finds for that era. It is generally assumed that the inhabitants of Catalonia clung to their Megalithic and Bell Beaker cultures well into the Bronze Age. The contrast between the Argaric development and the backwardness of Catalan industry throws into high relief how natural resources conditioned life of people, a point made most brilliantly just recently by Felipe Fernández-Armesto in the way he wrote his history of civilizations. [21] Also, while important Bronze Age sites have been found in the Balearic Islands, some reflecting Argaric influence, they raised important questions about possible sources even from the Middle East. Most important for our purposes, Catalonia's cultural life during the Bronze Age once again suggested that this region was undergoing changes different from Castilian Spain. The evidence for this conclusion continued to accumulate with time.

The coming of the Iron Age with its mass movement of people through the Rhine River area down to the Rhône River, and eventually into Catalonia, marked another era. The Celts were closely identified with the Urnfield people and are often mentioned in that way even in regard to Spanish Catalonia. Their custom of cremation and disposing of the ashes in urns subsequently buried in specific areas reserved for this purpose, proved to be the outstanding characteristic of these Iron Age people. Unfortunately, cremation left few skeletons which would enable anthropologists to determine racial characteristics and relationships.

Another problem concerned whether the discovery of urnfields and artifacts in a particular place dating from the Halstatt or La Tène times is sufficient evidence of a Celtic presence, or whether one has to assume that the region may have been occupied by indigenous tribes which forcibly or voluntarily adopted Celtic culture. Possibly, Celtic and local tribes may have existed side-by-side, each with a different level of civilization in the same epoch. In Spain these kinds of dilemmas led some to dub as post-Hallstattian developments in areas which were not fully in the La Tène phase, but bordered regions where the latter clearly dominated. For instance, post-Hallstatt stations have been found in Catalan and Aragonese hinterlands corresponding to a period when La Tène influences predominated in Catalonia.

Celtiberian people established themselves in Galicia, in

northeastern Spain and in the plateau of central Iberia in a similar mix. Evidence for the latter group also came from Roman accounts of military operations against the Celtiberians who considered themselves as such. [22] Some question remains regarding who were the inhabitants of Catalonia by the time the Greeks had established the trading colonies of Ampurias and Rhodes, probably in the first half of the fourth century BC.[23] For that matter, who were the Iberians, Ligurians, Illyrians, Tarteasians and "Celts" mentioned by early Greco-Roman chroniclers, basing their stories on reports made by Greek explorers and seafaring traders? Such questions remain largely unanswered for the entire peninsula, let alone for Catalonia, despite the remarkable contributions made by philologists, anthropologists, and archaeologists in recent years.

In fact, many of the names mentioned in the early texts could have referred only to geographical identifications without necessarily involving tribal or racial distinctions. Iberia, for example, could have been an area which included Celts, Ligurians, and Catalans among others, from the Rhône to the Ebro—a vast area taking in German, French, and Spanish regions. The Greeks dealt only with coastal peoples, such as the Catalans and their southern neighbors, and had little if any means of contacting the quarrelsome tribes in the interior of present-day Castile. The wall between Castilian tribes and Greek colonies, constructed out of poor communications and transportation infrastructures, was evident because it insulated many developments in Catalonia from those in the interior of Spain. It, therefore, is understandable why records from Ampurias, for instance, indicate that relations with neighboring indigenous tribes and among themselves were not always the best. Even the Romans confused references to the peoples of Spain until the Romanization process was well under way.[24] Thus, the problem of names goes far to explain why historians often blend Catalan and Castilian prehistory into one jumble of mixed facts and myths.[25]

Celtic Invasions

The people whom one may loosely term the "Celts" entered Catalonia in two distinct waves several hundred years apart. The first group came through the eastern tip of the Pyrenees sometime in the ninth or eighth century B.C. These early invaders, few in numbers, probably settled in the plateau and lowlands of the provinces of Gerona, Barcelona, and Tarragona, mainly on the Mediterranean side of the Sierra de la Llena towards the coast. The Celtic vanguard reached the Ebro as its farthest point of invasion. From the location of their urnfields, they were probably settled agriculturalists rather than pastoral people.

The second Celtic invasion of the Iberian Peninsula was massive and occurred in successive waves between the seventh and fifth centuries B.C., making contacts with the Greeks throughout the entire period and especially by the sixth century B.C. In contrast with the first urnfield invaders, the later Celts were apparently a pastoral people who crossed the Pyrenees from one end to the other through the easily negotiated passes. In Catalonia they also moved through most of the passes in the mountains as well as by the eastern tip. A puzzling circumstance in the Spanish Catalan area is the relative absence of Celtic place names. It could be that the drive into Catalonia was transitional in nature, since these later waves penetrated the whole of the Ebro valley and also moved deeply into the plains of Castile. As a result of comparisons with urnfield sites in southern France and northern Italy, we know that Celtic culture in Spain corresponded to the middle and late stages of the Hallstatt epochs.

The second period of Iron Age culture in Spain, known as the La Tène stage, became synonymous with what many called the Iberian Period. By the time that La Tène had become part of the Spanish cultural pattern, although admittedly a minor one, two simultaneous developments occurred affecting the Celts. One group of Celts blended with the tribes of the central plateau of Spain, becoming the later Celtiberians. Others were not infused with local Iberian cultural influences yet lost their identity as Celts. Thus, for many modern historians writing about this period, the term "Iberian" implied all the inhabitants of the peninsula regardless of race. To confuse matters even more, it should be remembered that the Greeks and Romans came to use "Iberian" also in this convenient if inaccurate sense. Whether there ever actually existed an Iberian homogeneous race or culture prior to the era of recorded history is still an enigma, despite much misinformed Spanish rhetoric to the contrary.

Perhaps if known Iberian writings could ever be deciphered, the answer to this riddle might be learned.

In Catalonia the Hallstatt Era extended well into the fourth century B.C. A more homogeneous culture which might be called something verging on Iberian in scope did not set roots in Catalonia until at least the third century B.C. when transportation and commerce allowed for increased contacts among various communities throughout the Iberian Peninsula. This view is supported by findings of buckles, pottery and other ceramic ware, metal implements and arms, and art objects and jewelry. Further evidence for this contention comes from the cyclopean design of walls surrounding indigenous towns and the urnfield nature of the Catalan necropolis. Most of the important Catalan Iberian sites were located along the Costa Brava, extending well into southern France along the Mediterranean coast, and reflected once again on the corridor nature of the passes at the eastern end of the Pyrenees.

Conclusions

With the establishment of the Celtic elements in Catalonia, the region's prehistory proper comes to an end. During the preceding period of approximately 235,000 years, the area which historians and local inhabitants would eventual know as Spanish Catalonia developed almost independently of other parts of the Iberian Peninsula. During this epoch, the Catalan region served as a cultural conduit into Spain. To a far lesser degree, some traffic northward into the rest of Europe occurred. A combination of factors amongst which one might include geographic, demographic, and culture accounted for the birth of Catalan regionalism. Events in later centuries built further points of differences and conflicts between modern Catalans and their Castilian neighbors, creating a political and cultural awareness in north-eastern Spain profoundly affecting the course of Iberian history down to the present. However, we should not overstate the case. In the earliest centuries of human occupation of what eventually became known as Catalonia, there was no regional nationalism or sense of identity. In fact even localism was probably not a feature of local culture until inhabitants became sedentary, and even then, perhaps strictly inward looking with little or no sense of bonds with other groups of humans until commercial interactions and the sharing of common languages began to emerge.

However, what must be taken very seriously are the natural effects of geography and climate. The fact that there were passes humans could traverse in a reasonable fashion, or that there were rivers and valleys that could sustain life, and even the availability of caves to protect one from the elements were crucial to the mundane tasks of humans moving about in search of food, shelter, and safety. Catalonia had all those elements and thus attracted people and served as an important north/south conduit into and out of the Iberian Peninsula. Second, climatic conditions proved conducive as well. Had the entire area been under a massive ice glacier for hundreds of thousands of years, this essay would have told a very different story. Again, conditions were conducive for human habitat, and for animals and plants to thrive of the kind that could sustain human life. In fact, there were enough natural resources that very early on humans could rise above the needs for food and shelter, and begin to make or acquire jewelry and perform decorated funerals and thus enjoy some of the "finer things of life," but which are important as sources of culture and civilization.

CHAPTER TWO
ROMANIZATION OF CATALONIA

Historians have paid an extraordinary amount of attention to the Roman period in Spanish history because of the importance and extent of Romanization that took place. Catalonia was not immune to the historic influences of the Roman world and, indeed, local culture and society evolved as a direct result. But there is an explicit reason to look at this history of Iberian Romanization, and in particular the case of Catalonia, because nations develop a predisposition towards law and public administration which eventually result in tilts in the direction of particular kinds of government and political philosophy. These phenomena are deeply rooted in the dim past of peoples or nations from which continuous threads survive through the ages that help to characterize a community as distinct or similar to others. In the case of the Iberian Peninsula, nowhere did Roman legal and institutional influence remain the longest than in Catalonia. To answer the obvious question about what about southern Spain, where Roman inheritance had set deeper roots, the long Islamic occupation of the region resulted in the elimination of most Latinized vestiges.

Roman presence had a profound effect on the Celtiberian and other Hispanic indigenous peoples to such a degree that contemporary attitudes reflect consequences of the Romanization of the peninsula. It took the Romans some two hundred years to pacify the peninsula, in contrast to only ten years in Gaul (essentially modern France).

Rome's direct involvement with the Iberian Peninsula extended over six hundred years. Initially, this interest stemmed from security issues related to the Punic wars. After the destruction of Carthage, economic objectives sparked the eventual subjugation of the entire peninsula, a process that itself required two hundred years to accomplish. Exploitation of natural resources, including manpower for its armies, tied the entire peninsula's destiny to that of Rome.

Romanization of Iberia proved to be a gradual phenomenon and varied greatly in extent and intensity. Along the Mediterranean coast and in the fertile Guadalquivir and Guadiana valleys, for instance, Roman language and customs supplanted local ways of life. In short, these areas became as Roman as Rome itself. But the deeper into Iberia the Romans went, the weaker was the cultural transformation brought by them. Best estimates placed the population of Roman *Hispania* at some 7 million people at about 180 A.D. That meant the population was both large but also dispersed across the large peninsula of 229,000 square miles. [1] Following pacification during the Augustinian era (318 B.C.-14 A.D.), the local Roman troops, who had settled and intermarried in Catalonia and elsewhere, were joined by Italian immigration, particularly along coastal regions, of all kinds lured by reports of natural bounties awaiting exploitation and a growing local economy.

Initial Roman Presence

For centuries prior to the arrival of Romans in Iberia other peoples from around the Mediterranean interacted with the Iberians. To get quickly to our story of the Roman influence, by 654 B.C. Carthage had developed a strong and important base in Ibiza, the smallest of the Ballearic islands off the coast of Catalonia. In time the Phoenicians who had remained in Tartessos in southern Iberia had sought aid from other kingdoms of the period, providing the excuse for the Carthaginian entry into southern Spain and that would eventually draw the Romans into the peninsula. Meanwhile in the north Greek colonies expanded from the northeast into central Iberia.

According to Pliny the Elder, the Roman historian who served in Spain as Procurator when the Romanization process was in full progress, the Greek city of Emporium was one tenth the size of an adjacent Iberian city. The later Roman city began as a military camp. Conducive to a close relationship between the Greeks and the Iberians of the northeast corner of the peninsula was a somewhat similar approach to government in terms of the city-state concept with its intrinsic democratic mold. Probably nearby Iberian tribes must have been affected to some degree by the clearly defined legal practices which dominated Greek political and administrative thought and by the intense commercial spirit which animated Greek life. One could speculate that perhaps Catalonia's long established reputation as a region of outstanding merchants can be traced back to early Greek influence in the region between the Ebro and the Pyrenees. An important Phocaean contribution to the economy along the coast was their introduction of wine vineyards and olive trees. Both wine and olive oil soon became important export products which encouraged the development of a mercantile community.

Excavations at the Iberian city of Ullastret, some nine miles from Emporium, revealed the extent of Greek commercial influence in the area believed to have been occupied by the native Indikete tribes. The earliest foundations of the city rested on rock and judging from the artifacts found in the first layers uncovered, the origins of Ullastret must have been around the sixth century B.C. Throughout Gerona province and reasonably near Ullastret, numerous sites have been found reflecting the early invasion of th Urnfield people and corresponding Hallstatt finds mixed with clearly indigenous or pre-Celtic objects. For that stage of cultural development there was a total absence of Greek objects. Cermaics found in some parts of Ullastret conformed to the Hallstatt era characteristic of the region. At a later stage the first items of Greek imports were located in relative abundance. Gray deramic ware from Asia Minor, Ionian ceramics, Etruscan vases, amphoras, and many other products of the early sixth century suggested the extent of Phocaean economic efforts in Catalonia with Emporium and Rhodes as points of entry. In explorations conducted in the Gulf of Rosas in 1938 by Fernando Cufí in search of the Rhodian ruins, Iberian imitations of Ionic-Phocaean ceramic of the fifth century B.C. or even earlier were found, clear evidence of the influence of the Greeks on Iberian industry, even at that early period.[2]

Excavations in Ullastret showed that the city was most densely populated in the fifth to thire centuries B.C. Findings for these periods closely resembled those discovered throughout the prince of Gerona for the same era. Interestingly and inexplicably, the diggers at Ullastret failed to uncover products of Italian origin for the period immediately following the Roman landings at Emporium in 217 B.C. Other Iberian centers received a substantial flow of Italian imports which followed the Roman troops. Ullastret might have been destroyed during the campaigns against Iberian tribes north of the Ebro led by Roman general Marcus Porcius Cato the Elder, in 195 B.C. Also found at Ullastret were coins of Punic origin proving that considerable intracoastal trade must have taken place despite rivalries between the Carthaginians and the Phocaeans.

Beyond the coastal regions there existed in Iberia little influenced by Carthaginians or Greeks. The hinterland was inhabited by innumerable separate clans, each linked closely within its group in extended family relationships, and usually centered in a fortified town or city. These tribes were fiercely jealous of their independence with war as an important pastime. Loyalties shifted according to circumstances of the moment with lasting alliances a rarity. For centuries Phoenicians and Carthagenians drew heavily on the Iberian tribes as mercenaries. Later under Rome, after the pacification of the peninsula, they became important factors in the conquests beyond Italy and Iberia.

Punic Wars

The First Punic War began as a conflict for control of Sicily between the Romans and the Carthagenians. It began in 264 B.C. and lasted for twenty-three years. This and the other conflict with the Carthagenians had profound repercussions for the Catalans and the Iberians because Roman power went international and spread across the Mediterranean world. So, in the first war, Carthage was stopped from taking Sicily and in the process, Rome became a naval power. Subsequently, Carthage turned its interests more inwardly in the Iberian Peninsula. As part of its expansion into the peninsula, the Carthagenians established a fortified center called Barcino, which eventually came to be known as Barcelona. However, the Carthaginians found it difficult, indeed impossible, to hold onto territories north of the Ebro because of constant tribal hostility. But the threat to what someday would be Catalonia of Carthaginian intrusions remained.

The Phocaeans at Emporium and Massalia were aware that they would be easy targets for Carthaginian conquest, and thus fully shared Rome's fears and objectives in Spain. As Catalan historian Ferran Soldevila aptly argued, Rome saw in the area between the Ebro and the Pyrenees, that is Catalonia, a buffer zone or march, much in the same manner in which the Carolingians viewed this region when Islam threatened southern France in the ninth and tenth centuries.[3]

In 218 B.C. the famed Hannibal, then a young Carthaginian commander, invaded north of the Ebro thereby precipitating the Second Punic War (218-201 B.C.). Eager to keep the Carthaginians from fighting Romans in Italy or Sicily, the Roman Senate decided to meet Carthage in the Iberian Peninsula. Local residents at Emporium and nearby supported fully local Roman intentions and armed forces, and provided military auxiliaries as well. As a result, the Roman position was consolidated at Emporium and they held the line at the Ebro River. With additional Roman reinforcements soon after, a military headquarters was established at Tarraco (known today as Tarragona), then pushed across the river along the coast towards Sagunto which fell to them in 212 B.C.

Most of the war was fought south of the Ebro River and finally in 211 B.C. the Carthaginians forced the Romans back across the river, essentially returning the situation to what it had been in 217 B.C. when the Romans occupied the territory north of the river and the Carthaginians to the south. Additional Roman troops, freed up from warfare in Italy, started coming into Catalonia in 21 B.C. and in the following year this strong army, also reinforced by local Iberians, attacked New Carthage (Cartagena). The Roman army took over the city, which was one of the finest ports in the Mediterranean region and had serviced as the Carthaginian provincial capital. The Carthaginians now retreated southward to what is today Cadiz, which fell to the Romans in 206 B.C., resulting in the final withdrawal of the Carthiginians from the Iberian Peninsula. To close out the story, Romans invaded North Africa, defeating Carthiginian forces in 202 B.C., ending the Second Punic War, eliminating Carthage as a military power, and with all of the Iberian Peninsula coming under Roman control along with Sicily and all of North Africa. Rome was now a world super power.

Early Romanization of Iberia and Catalonia

At this point Rome became deeply involved with an Iberia about which it had only limited knowledge. The Romans were familiar with the situation along the Levant coastal areas and what is now Andalusia, but, were quite ignorant about the rest of Spain, including Catalonia. On the Catalan coast in the vicinity of Emporium, and in most of Gerona province, Indiketes and Ausetani tribes operated and lived. To their south in the region of Barcelona lived the Layetani. The Edetani people occupied land immediately below the Ebro delta, while the Ilergetas held the Catalan hinterland. In the south central section of the Pyrenees and towards the plateaus beyond the foothills of the Pyrenees and towards the plateaus beyond the foothills to the Ebro were the Vascones. A similar litany of various tribes could be told about the rest of Spain. The point to keep in mind is that all of these tribes in varying degrees of strength stood between Rome and the complete conquest of any area, let alone all of Iberia.

Consequently, the Romanization of the different regions occurred at various speeds and in different periods. Tribal customs and characteristics also affected the blend of the indigenous way of life with that of the Romans. In some instances, for example, Roman legionaries married Iberian women and these mixed marriages helped considerably to Latinize the Iberians. In fact, the term Romanization is really a misnomer since most of the Roman soldiers came from different parts of Italy and so too brought with them various customs, manners, and speech that differed from those of true Romans.

There were cities established primarily for Roman veterans and citizens such as Italica in Andalusia, which were, in essence, small replicas of Rome. In other instances there were Iberian towns and cities which kept their own identities, but endeavored to imitate the dominant power and culture, and in time became thoroughly Romanized. With successive generations of Iberians also serving in the legions, the Romanization of Hispania grew apace. By the time of Caesar Augustus, Iberians in the coastal regions and in large parts of Andalusia (called Baetica at the time) no longer clung to their native speech or way of life. Tarragona and New Carthage, for example, were now thoroughly Roman. The advent of the Romans with a legal and administrative system and philosophy which mirrored importations from Greece eased the process in areas such as the two mentioned and other parts of Iberia and Catalonia.

The establishment by Cneius Scipio of his army's headquarters at Tarraco in 218 B.C. contributed greatly towards the rapid Latinization of Catalonia. The existence of Greek culture in the Catalan area, which was occidental and hence similar to Rome's furthered the adoption of Roman ways by the coastal Iberians. It was no accident, therefore, that Tarragona became the first of the Iberian cities to become thoroughly Roman, complete to its architectural forms, life styles, and culture. On the other hand, as the Romans drove further inland, Latinization came about more slowly.

In the period roughly 205 B.C. to 200 B.C., the two most important Ilerget chieftains in the Catalan hinterland—Indivil and Mandonius—rebelled against Roman suzerainty with the support of the Ausetani and Layetani tribes from the eastern coastal zone. Indivil died in battle, the Romans captured Mandonius and executed him, and the uprising ended.

Despite this Roman victory, an atmosphere of widespread unrest continued, caused by the severe methods of taxation implemented by the Roman governors and their exorbitant collections, much of which went into their personal coffers. This system was abusive mainly because Roman senior officials obtained remuneration primarily from tax proceeds. The practice remained in effect until the era of Augustus who established a policy of fixed salaries for government officials throughout the Empire.

During the early phases of Roman conquest (to be specific, in 197 B.C.), following the destruction of Carthage, Rome divided its Spanish conquests into two administrative divisions. The organization and administrative patterns developed at the time survived until the reign of Caesar Augustus (27 B.C.-14 A.D.) when a major reorganization was undertaken throughout the Empire. The precise location of the original dividing line between Hispania Citerior (Hither Spain) and Hispania Ulterior (Father Spain) remains uncertain. Citerior, or Hither province, covered

23

approximately the general area which had long been in contact with visiting Phoceaean Greeks from Marssalis (modern day Marseilles) and those living in Emporium, as well as their small trading colonies to the south on the coast under direct Roman control after the Second Punic War. Ulterior, or Farther Province, was largely the region previously under Carthaginian control. The reason for this peculiar division of the newly won territories was due largely to Rome's lack of detailed knowledge of Hispania's geography and its people much beyond the coastal trips.

Between 196 B.C. and 194 B.C., Cato the Elder faced almost continuous conflict with Iberian tribes all over Hispania. Extant evidence suggests that he landed initially at Emporium, because the Greek Phocaeans were the only friends Rome had at the time. It appears that insurrection in the Catalan region was almost total among the local tribes, and extended into the central plateaus. By adroit diplomacy, bribery, and outstanding military action, Cato subdued the Catalan tribes.[4] During his administration, Rome clashed for the first time with the Celtiberians on their own soil. Cato also pushed Roman conquest well into Aragon, capturing Salduvia (Caesar Augustus, "Zaragoza," and Osca, "Huesca"). He not only subjugated the Catalan and Aragonese regions, but also the area south of the Ebro as far as Almanzora in Andalusia.

Rome continued to face difficult times in Hispania. From the time of Cato's departure from Spain in 194 B.C. to the arrival in Tarragona of Tiberius Sempronius Gracchus in 178 B.C., Rome faced the problem of subduing rebellions all over the peninsula, including fighting Lusitanians and Celtiberians without conclusive results. Some of its generals and governors were more competent than others, but none could achieve more than passing victories. Roman officials still implemented a policy of exploiting its Iberian territories to the utmost while the fighting continued. But the gain in gold and silver extracted from Hispania was more than offset by the drain on Roman materiel and human resources. Between 205 B.C. and 179 B.C., Rome sent 70,000 troops and deployed an additional 80,000 Latin allies in its troublesome provinces.[5] Until Iberius Gracchus assumed responsibility for Citerior in 181 B.C., none of his many predecessors, with the possible exception of Cato, approached the Iberian problem in terms of a comprehensive policy with long range views as a intrinsic factor.

A period of effective management of the Iberian holdings made for a time of relative peace lasting until 154 B.C. During this long era of relative quiet Romanization of the two Iberian provinces accelerated. Many Celtiberian communities became *socii*, or allies, of Rome. Consequently, commercial activities greatly intensified between the metropolis and the Spanish provinces. Tarragona and the other principal cities on the coast prospered and acquired increasingly a Roman character.

Iberian Rebellions

But then Roman rule entered a new phase, one marked by many local rebellions. The political intrigue, military campaigns, and form of Roman administration catalogued the last profoundly important resistance to the Romanization of Iberia. The details of these revolts suggested the extent of Roman penetration and influence. The ultimate defeat of the Iberian tribes ushered in an era in which Roman customs were permanently ingrained into the Spanish social structure, if one could even refer monolithically to a single culture. Revolts and battles raged for years all over the Iberian Peninsula, including in northeast Spain. Roman armies experienced many difficulties, including lost battles, generals humiliated, great expenses, and political turmoil for Rome. In 134 B.C. things came to a head when Scipio Aemilianus arrived in Tarragona with fresh Roman troops. He imposed military discipline on the demoralized local Roman army and laid siege to Numantia. Facing starvation the Numantians set fire to their city and committed mass suicide. For two thousand years afterwards, the story of the fall of Numantia was often told, taking on near-mythic proportions in local history. Dramatics aside, however, the fall of Numantia meant that the intense Romanization of Spain could now take place and be completed. With the hindsight of time and history, that process now appeared inevitable.

Romanization After Numantia

After the events at Numantia, the destiny of the Iberian Peninsula became linked indissolubly with that of Rome. The Republic's civil wars had repercussions in Spain with Celtiberians in Citerior taking sides, even fighting in Italy. In 1908 a bronze plaque found in Italy revealed that, as a reward for their performance in Rome's Social War (98-89 B.C.), a cavalry unit from Salduba (Zaragoza) received Roman citizenship. Iberian names on this plaque documented their participation in the Italian campaigns.

After the destruction of Numantia, immigration from Italy increased. These permanent settlers consisted of merchants, former or present government officials, demobilized Roman soldiers, returned Latinized Iberian troops, Italian laborers, mining and industrial technicians. Within a relatively short time along the coast in urban centers, Latin supplanted Iberian dialects. Roman dress, customs, and religion also became the way of life. Roman architecture and construction prevailed. Most important, Roman concepts of law and government administration became firmly grafted on new or transformed political bodies. Trade in Iberia increased with the construction of a road along the coast from the Pyrenees to New Carthage. Tarragona flourished immensely as did Italica in the south. Tribes in the interior were affected considerably less by the large increase in Roman population. Thus, the Romanization process not only took much longer to develop in the inland regions, but never acquired the depth of influence characteristic of the coast. This circumstance is probably one of the remote, yet important, reasons for eventual differences centuries later in the outlook towards empire, trade, law, and government between landlocked Castile, the Basque provinces, and the highly Latinized predominantly coastal Catalonia.

After the fall of Numantia in 133 B.C., Iberia's participation in Rome's affairs intensified. Between the destruction of Numantia and the collapse of the Roman republic in 31. B.C., when Octavius (later named Caesar Augustus) triumphed over Mark Anthony and Cleopatra, two important events occurred affecting Iberia. One stemmed from political rivalry within Rome itself. Quintus Sartorius, a Roman general with lofty political aspirations, established a base in Spain for rebellion against the imperial order. Between 82 B.C. and 72 B.C. he successfully resisted imperial forces, even going to the extreme of creating a Roman Senate and school at Osca (Huesca in northern Aragon). Since members of both institutions were mostly native Iberians, the effects of Sartorius' action contributed to the Romanization of Central Spain. When he was assassinated, however, his rebellion collapsed.

Quintus Sartorius' revolt in Iberia did not develop on behalf of any national Iberian independence, but for the establishment of a Roman government in Spain led by a Roman general. Sartorius considered Iberia as an integral part of the Roman polity. To establish a new government in Iberia from his point of view would have been no different than doing so in Rome or elsewhere in Italy. For that reason his actions are important to any understanding of Roman influence in Iberia.

Born near Rome, Sartorius was an enfranchised Italian who, through courage and military skill, rose to prominence in the Roman army. In the intense conflicts between the popular party in Rome led by Gaius Marius, who had risen from the lowest ranks of society to the consulship, and the aristocratic oligarchy represented by Lucius Cornelius Sulla, Sartorius sided with Marius. As a young officer, Sartorius had served in Iberia. At the time of the Marius-Sulla civil war, Sartorius returned to Hispania on the former's behalf and quickly secured the region for Marius. However, in 81 B.C., when Sulla achieved supremacy in Rome, his troops broke Sartorius' grip in the peninsula. The following year the Lusitani invited Sartorius to lead a general revolt, an offer which he accepted. For ten years until assassinated by his deputy, Sartorius kept Rome at bay.

In his attempt to create an Iberian-based Roman republic, Sartorius organized his capital at Huesca. He established a school for the sons of local Iberian chiefs, and his Senate of 300 was comprised of prominent followers of Marius. In justification of his actions he maintained that Sulla ruled illegally as an usurper and tyrant and that, therefore, the Spanish regime was the caretaker of Rome's traditional institutions. From Huesca Sartorius conducted international relations with sympathetic kings and magnates as far away as Asia Minor. Meanwhile, his educational efforts at Huesca furthered the Romanization of Spain.

Historian Francis J. Wiseman observed aptly that, "it is indeed tempting to suggest that, aware of the grave constitutional weaknesses in a city-state controlling a world-wide empire, he intended to apply those remedial measures that Caesar was to employ some thirty years later."[6] Quite likely, Sartorius did think along those lines as evidenced by the steps he took at Huesca. But as Wiseman further noted, "he failed to forge an army strong enough as a weapon for his hand," a mistake not repeated by Julius Caesar several decades later.[7] Yet, the Sartorius movement had the effect of heightening a sense of Iberian identification with Rome and its internal political problems.

The second event affecting the course of Catalan evolution concerned a passing but serious invasion of Iberia by barbarian German tribes in 104 B.C., a circumstance which led to the Iberians taking the initiative to repel successfully this assault. The Cimbri and Teutons, reportedly over 300,000 in total numbers, erupted into western Europe from their homeland in northeastern Europe (probably Jutland) where increased population exerted excessive pressure on their lands. They threatened Rome's hold in Gaul and at one point the very existence of the capital itself. They destroyed two Roman armies near Orange in Provence on the French side of the Pyrenees in 105 B.C. These defeats (resulting in over 80,000 Roman casualties) encouraged the barbarians to invade Iberia. With some 30,000 warriors, they chose to enter the peninsula through the easern end of the Pyrenees in the vicinity of modern Puigcerda in Gerona province. This action brought the invaders into direct confrontation with the Celtiberians who, after Numantia, had remained remarkably quiet. What the Roman legions failed to do the Celtiberians achieved. Resorting to their traditional tactics of harassment and guerrilla warfare, they wore down the Germanic tribes forcing them to recross the mountains and return to Gaul.

Emboldened by their success, the Celtiberians in Citerior once more staged an uprising against the Romans but without the dimensions of their pre-Numantian efforts. Rome assigned Consul Titus Didius to Citerior in 98 B.C. to suppress these new revolts. It took five years to destroy the Celtiberian resistance. Taking advantage of Rome's difficulties, the Lusitani also rose in rebellion in Ulterior in an uncoordinated movement, but they too were subjugated by 93 B.C., leaving Roman Spain quiet once more. With the end of this fighting, Rome's position in Spain became definitively clearer.

Over two hundred years of continuous wars of conquest had netted the Romans control of the Mediterranean area and vast regions in Europe proper, such as Iberia and parts of southern France. But this expansion depleted Italian manpower with a consequent weakening of the independent farmer class—the backbone of the Roman state. The gradual disappearance in Italy of small farms and the emergence of immensely wealthy large landowners, drawing heavily on virtually inexhaustible supplies of slaves for labor, drove into the capital ever growing masses of former, now landless, farmers who had been unable to compete for jobs in the slave-ridden countryside. The massive acquisition of booty, particularly gold and silver, permitted capitoline Rome to subsidize welfare programs for the vast number of unemployed citizenry in order to avoid violent outbreaks. One other consequence of Rome's extraordinary successes and the acute weakening of civic virtue affected affected the Senate, a body in which practically "everything" had a price tag. It thus became only a question of time before emerging governmental ineptitude and corruption sounded the death knell for the Republic, paving the way for Octavius' ascent to power.

Iberian participation in Rome's internal affairs was further intensified through involvement in the struggle by Julius Caesar against Pompey for control of the Republic. Ultimately, after a four year campaign, his defeat of Pompey's sons at Munda in 45 B.C. in the southern province settled the issue and made Caesar ruler of the Roman world.

Augustinian Administration and Law

Octavius' ascent to power as Caesar Augustus was an event of extraordinary and far-reaching importance not only for the Roman world, but also for the destiny of Europe, a fact acknowledged by historians writing about the period over hundreds of years. Therefore, there is no need to analyze in close detail the Augustan Era, but certain aspects which impinged on Iberia's evolution do warrant attention, particularly as they pertain to the evolution of Catalonia.

Caesar Augustus brought to power unusually good administrative skills and talent, combined with considerable ability in dealing with a Senate which had long abandoned the sturdy virtues and ideals characteristic of its earlier days. But Augustus also envisioned realistically a global policy for Rome's future, a knack rare in statesmen in any era. Forged in an atmosphere of deadly intrigue and treachery, Augustus emerged from his struggle for survival and power with two important traits: the ability to appoint capable leaders and to assure their personal loyalty.

The Augustan Era, correctly called the "principate," because of Octavius' designation by the Senate of *princeps* (first citizen), was based on the theory that Rome was a republic with the Senate still the governing authority. In accepting the total powers "thrust" upon him by the Senate, Octavius, however, gradually converted the solons from a legislative body to a consultative function. His successor, Tiberius (14-37 A.D.), cast off any pretense at recognizing the Senate as the source of power. He functioned as emperor from the very beginning of his reign, a situation which remained until the eventual collapse of the empire.

The legitimacy of the new regime established by Augustus never became an issue, because it rested on a sound constitutional basis. The powers gathered into his hands stemmed from actions formally initiated in the Senate. Apart from the venality of the Senators, and whatever inducements might have indirectly flowed from Octavius, all Roman social classes, particularly the bankers and merchants (mostly from the *quites* or knights' class, intermediate between *nobiles* or nobles and plebians), were at the limits of their patience with the disorders arising from Julius Caesar's assassination. Furthermore, Roman expansion had reached a point requiring more efficient administration. By the time of Julius Caesar's death, Roman power engulfed all of Iberia except a small sector in the northwest corner and pockets of the Basque country, Gaul, all of Italy, Dalmatia, Greece, and extensive areas in Asia Minor and North Africa. This large conglomeration of nations and races proved too unwieldy to govern for a collective body such as the Senate.

Without detracting from Augustus' abilities, and despite corruption in the Senate, was a mark of Roman political genius that the complexity of the problem was understood. It was also clear that a method of succession had to be devised to assure smooth transition of power from one emperor to another; hence, the concentration of authority in a *princeps*. In principle the idea was not too far removed from that of dictatorship, an institution to which Romans resorted in the past when grave national danger led to concentration of power. The main difference was that dictators were appointed for the duration of the crisis, while Octavius' designation and that of his successors was for life.

Julius Caesar recognized the need to Romanize gradually conquered peoples of non-Italian origin in order to ease their absorption into the Roman whole. There existed ample precedent for the manner in which Roman expansion in Italy had assimilated the other city-states and non-Latin tribes. The basis for this development was the granting of certain rights to subjugated peoples, and to their cities and towns, in what amounted to a graduated scale dependent upon degrees of Romanization and genuine identification with Rome's interests.

The Iberian Peninsula was Rome's first experience with conquests outside of Italy. The initial military considerations gave way after the destruction of Carthage to lasting commercial, social, and political relationships, developments calling for improvement in the haphazard administration under the Senate in the Republican period. Caesar, during his involvement in Spain, for purposes both of personal advantage and benefit to Rome, consciously developed a policy designed to draw close Iberian identification with the Metropolis. The basis for his policy was the establishment of colonies reflecting Roman municipal life and organization. This approach permitted the strengthening of the Roman military presence and offered to the Iberians a model to emulate, including the Catalan region. The carrot of Roman citizenship was held out as the ultimate prize for thorough Romanization.

The establishment of municipalities was the instrument for the consolidation and eventual absorption of conquered territories and peoples. In fact, the entire empire eventually became a vast mass of cities connected by a splendid network of roads. There was certainly truth in the aphorism "all roads lead to Rome." In Spain the two props of Roman imperialism—municipalities and roads—were basic to governing Iberia. Regardless of the formula adopted for, or by, any particular area, Rome retained for itself ultimate domination.

Another factor of importance in the process of urbanization was the significance of citizenship already suggested. Apart from the prestige (which was important), there were tangible benefits derived from such status. Roman citizens could not be mistrusted or punished unless tried in a Roman court. When threatened with a death sentence, the citizen could "appeal to Caesar" against a presumed unjust judgment, as did St. Paul. Citizenship conferred voting rights, eligibility to hold public office and legal validity of marriage with inheritance implications for the progeny. In a crude age, these alone among many were of great importance. One attitude or approach for indigenous groups wishing to move in the direction of such advantages was to mimic as closely as possible Roman municipal organization and physical characteristics (coliseums, architecture, public works, language, and customs). Rome demonstrated great flexibility in regard to the variety of municipal concepts it encouraged or tolerated.

Roman notion held that a municipality could include large estates and extensive territory beyond its actual walls or urban limits, including villages and hamlets. Within Italy the term municipality (*municipium*) in its legal sense had come to mean any urban center granted a charter by Rome, which enjoyed as a minimum Latin Rights (*jus Latii*). These concerned originally in the main the area between Etruria and Campagna, the latter the low plain around ancient Rome. Under the *jus Latii*, subjected cities were considered "friends and allies of the Roman people." Although through defeat they had lost the freedom to declare war, the making of treaties and mintage rights, they nonetheless were left with liberty to govern themselves. They could engage in commerce under Rome's patronage and were generally exempt from payment of tribute. In the early days of the Republic, their main obligation was to furnish troops when so required. Long after the Italian cities which enjoyed Latin Rights had either disappeared or been absorbed thoroughly into the Roman polity, the concept in the basic *jus Latii* perdured as part of the Roman formula in its policies of expansion in Spain and elsewhere. Cartaya (in the province of modern Huelva) in Spain was founded in 171 B.C. on the basis of *jus Latii* for Roman soldiers or veterans of the Plebeian class. As the Republic matured and expanded, *jus Italicum* became the more generalized formula. Under this doctrine, municipalities were under direct Roman control even if they elected their own magistrates, and all paid Rome at least the *vectigal*, a tax levied on a district but not individually. Rome considered all conquered lands as belonging to the public, or rather more precisely, as state domain and as such subject to taxation.

By the time of Emperor Vespasian (70-79 A.D.), there were more than 300 towns and cities in Spain and they included a very wide variety of communities. Some were *civitates stipendiariae* ("tributary" towns) subject to considerable taxation. In contrast, there were a few towns, possibly not more than a half dozen,[8] known as *civitates immunes* ("exempted" towns) free of tax payment and obligated only to assist Roman magistrates in whatever manner requested. They had their own laws and did not benefit from the *jus Italicum* or other particular privileges. There also were *civitatis faederatae* ("allied" cities) with which Rome had treaty arrangements. Generally, their main obligation consisted of supporting Rome in a military fashion. The most important of the municipalities were *coloniae* (settlements) formed by Roman citizens and founded essentially as military outposts or bases. These kinds of towns and cities had precedents dating to the very early times of Roman expansion at the expense of their Latin neighbors. Yet another category of communities was that of *civitates liberae* ("free" cities) about which little is known regarding their degree of independence from Rome and which could be easily confused with the *civitatis faederatae*. Communities not necessarily populated by Roman citizens, but which still enjoyed Roman rights, were referred to as *municipia* (provincial town or city). There were also numerous *municipium civium romanorum* (cities of Roman citizens). Many, if not most, of the urban centers which received Rome's blessings in one form or another still exist in modern Spain as cities, towns, or hamlets.

The system of roads created in Spain for military and commercial purposes proved of extraordinary importance both as to quality of construction and routes selected. To a considerable extent the network served as the basis for the road linkages built or modernized in the peninsula over the last two hundred years.[9]

In broad terms Augustus transformed the organization of the Principate into a highly centralized system leading to him as the source of power. He established a standing army which looked to him as commander-in-chief with the prospect of rewards stemming from Augustus as *imperator*. They looked to Augustus, and to his successors, for honorable discharges, which led to pensions and often to grants of land. At the peak of Roman power in the second century A.D., there were 25 legions which, when added to auxiliary forces, provided Rome with a military might in excess of some 300,000 men under arms. They guarded all the frontiers, built walls for defense, roads, aqueducts, and bridges.

Augustus divided all provinces into two basic groups. Those which were thoroughly pacified were placed under the jurisdiction of the Senate in Rome, but also indirectly his watchful eye through special delegates sent to look matters over from time-to-time. This was particularly his practice regarding the integrity of the tax and judicial systems. Areas requiring careful military presence, or had been newly conquered, came under the direct control of Augustus. His personal representatives governed these areas and Augustus followed closely their events. In time about three-quarters of all of Rome's approximately 43 provinces were directly responsible to the emperors. The Augustan governors administered local affairs, commanded the military, and functioned as judges in serious matters.

Of great importance to the provinces was the civil service system created by Augustus. Provincial government became characterized by the assignment of properly trained career administrators who were paid a fixed salary with the probability of a generous pension after retirement. This development led to a proliferation of the legal profession. Yet, the creation of a civil service was an improvement over previous arrangements, because it eliminated the gross corruption and mismanagement which had disgraced many of the politicians and untrained personnel assigned to the provinces by the Senate under the old system. Another consequence was a marked reduction throughout the Roman world in attempts at armed revolts arising from abuses by provincial governors.

Augustus also reformed the tax system. The collection of taxes was no longer farmed out to publicans, nor could governors willy nilly exort outrageous sums out of the provinces. Taxation was established on a fixed formula based on census data, while consideration was taken of property values in establishing these rates. Closely tied to this reform of the tax system was the innovation of a reliable postal system whereby official and commercial communications became possible based on dependable schedules.

Augustus strengthened the position of religion throughout the Principate through the reconstruction of temples, his encouragement of *concilia* (assemblies) as religious centers, and by raising the prestige of the office of *flamen* (priest).

In Spain, the division of the Principate into provinces resulted in Augustus retaining control of Citerior Hither province (renamed Tarraconensis) and assuming direct responsibility for the new province of Lusitania, split off from Baetica, which was retained by the Senate. Lusitania corresponded roughly to the geographical footprint of modern Portugal, but extended somewhat into Asturias and Galicia in Spain. This basic organization remained in place until the second century when Tarraconensis was subdivided into three parts. The northwest district became the province of Gallaecia, and to the south of Tarraconensis, east of Gallaecia and Lusitania, and north of Baetica (Andalusia), Carthaginensis was created with its main seat at New Carthage (Cartagena). The Balearic Islands, considered by Rome as part of Iberia, eventually became a province. In Constantine's reign (324-337 A.D.) the western part of North Africa was organized as the province of Mauritania Tingitana and became part of the diocese of Spain. Thus, by the end of the third century, there were seven Iberian provinces.

After the pacification of the northwest corner of Spain and the provinces' reorganization, three Roman legions were permanently settled in Iberia. What is certain is that from the Augustan Era until the early fifth century (some 400 years) Spain enjoyed extraordinary peace and prosperity. The only serious exception was the invasion by the Franks and Suevi (264-276 A.D.) along the northeastern coastal areas, destroying Tarraco and the countryside. But this was a passing storm not repeated until the barbarian Alani, Suevi, and Vandals swept into Spain in 409 A.D., at the time that Alaric and his Visigoths assaulted and sacked Rome.[10] Also, in about 172 A.D. and again in 175 A.D., important raids or actual attempts at invasion by North African Moors occurred without serious consequences.[11]

Roman Heritage

The salient fact which remains impressive is that for six hundred years, there had been an association steadily growing between Iberians and Romans or Italians. The Catalan region of Hispania was a central part of that story in the peninsula, from the moment when the Romans landed at Emporium to the invasion of Suevi, Alani, and Vandals. When one considers the significance of such a span of time, the question naturally arises concerning how much of the Roman or Italian ethos grafted permanently onto the Iberian psyche, and how great actually was the factor of intermingling through marriage or concubinage. That Roman administrative institutions, language, and law survived well into the Spain of the Middle Ages, and probably down to the present, is understandable.

Intertwined in the late vestiges of Romanization was the impact of Christianity. Here was a religion with tremendous moral, political, and organizational implications. Introduced into Spain at an early stage during the Roman period, it became a central component of Spanish identity and culture. While details of its introduction remain sketchy, tradition holds that St. Paul and St. James evangelized the peninsula. Early stories and myths about martyrs place them in Catalonia as well as in other parts of Iberia, but particularly in Romanized Baetica and Tarraconensis.[12] However, all that said, the Catholic Church played a more important role in Spanish society after Roman rule ended in Iberia.

Looking over the entire expanse of Roman presence in Iberia, one is led to conclude that neither the Roman Republic nor the Empire developed the concept of representational government as a means of managing the Romanized world. Instead, whether in the Republican Era when power centered in the Roman Senate, a pattern of centralization remained a key political characteristic of Roman history. Inherent in this fact was the authoritarian model developed in the governing of the provinces, beginning with Iberia, the first of Rome's non-Italian adventures of conquest. This trait was reinforced in Church administration after the Christianization of Iberia, and later in the consolidation of the Visigothic monarchy. Authoritarianism and rigidity, as intrinsic realities, also characterized the Muslim areas after Tarik's invasion in 711 A.D., a movement which resulted in an Arab (Moorish) presence in the peninsula of some eight hundred years.

Spanish scholars generally agreed that both Hispanic character and political experience reflected influences derived from the Roman, Visigothic, and Muslim occupations in the peninsula. The differences in opinion varied with regard to the predominance of which. Some believed that pre-Iberian attitudes were never completely obliterated from the Spanish psyche. Others referred to the probable persistence of Jewish influences, particularly in southern Spain.[13]

Regardless of how much these various cultures affected the subsequent evolution of Spanish culture and political dispositions, authoritarianism was part of the Roman inheritance.[14]

Catalonia retained vestiges of Roman influence for centuries. Physical remains of Roman occupation can still be found in Catalonia, while its legal traditions can be traced directly back to the Romans, and as carried forward by Visigoths and others who followed. Longer and often more intensely than many other parts of Iberia, Catalonia had been very Romanized and a half millennium of influence would be hard to shake off.

CHAPTER THREE
FROM ROMAN DECLINE TO THE RISE AND PASSAGE OF THE VISIGOTHIC ERA: THE EFFECTS ON CATALONIA

The very early history of Catalonia cannot be sufficiently understood without taking into account the events that took place at the end of the Roman era, extended through that of the Visigothic dominance, and that evolved into the early Christian states and the start of their long 700-year struggle to push the Moslems out of the Iberian Peninsula. The heart of what needs to be understood from this period as sources of Catalan political views and attitudes towards law and society are the local views towards authoritarianism and principles affecting law and the institutions of authority, such as the monarchy in Spain. Roman and Visigothic influences spread to all Spanish states, not just to the Catalans, from Roman to Visigothic rule to Frankish times, the latter which retained many Roman overtones recognized by so many historians who have studied the early Christian kingdoms.

The Roman heritage influenced the Visigothic to a considerable extent. The impact made up important threads which survived in the Christian kingdoms throughout the centuries of Islamic presence. Gradually, inherited political tendencies accompanied the Christian repopulation of Spain as Moslems were pushed back. In general, much of the Roman heritage retained in the Visigothic period affected profoundly church and governmental organization, legal institutions, and attitudes toward political authority.

Collapse of the Roman Empire

The collapse of the Roman Empire in the West was not a sudden affair, but rather the result of a transformation which lasted several centuries, culminating in the establishment of Germanic kingdoms in Italy, Gaul, and Spain. In short, the collapse was a far bigger event than the continued evolution of Catalonia. The Catalans were part of a much larger flow of events. Across the entire Empire, its demise was accompanied civil wars, growth of vast rural estates owned mostly by high ranking Roman or Romanized barbarian officials (with the consequent elimination or diminution of small and medium sized independent farms, particularly in Iberia), crushing tax burdens on the population in general, all of which contributed to the creation of vast numbers of rural proletariat communities irrevocably tied to land. These trends, and the phenomenon of links to the land, proved to be the case in general throughout the Empire. In Spain, by the time of the barbarian invasions, large tracts of land had been abandoned as owners found it impossible to meet fiscal obligations. Furthermore, a kind of pre-feudal situation evolved with clients and labor closely tied to the landowning magnates. How many rural workers were legally slaves and how many free is not known. Only in the northwestern mountainous corner of the peninsula and in the wilder regions of the Pyrenees did latifundia fail to take root.

Participation in commerce was socially an inferior profession for social and political elites. In fact, Roman law prohibited the powerful senatorial class, extended throughout the Empire, from engaging in such activities. Therefore, magnates spent their entrepreneurial energies on amassing as much land as possible as their way of pursuing wealth. With the gradual breakdown of law and order, large landowners formed what in effect were private armies for self-protection. While these could fend off petty brigandage, none were large enough to defend their communities, let alone larger areas in Iberia, against foreign invasion, nor did a mechanism exist any longer sufficiently effective for the unification of these private military resources. Nor did Rome have in place a sufficient number of well trained legions capable of defending crumbling frontiers and for maintaining internal stability.

Concomitant with the existence in Spain of large rural estates, particularly in central and southern Spain, and many belonging at the time of Emperor Honorius to his relatives, cities diminished sharply in importance. Imperial policy forced municipal governing classes to pay levied taxes whether a city, or individually as officials, could afford it or not. If necessary, the required funds came out of the private resources of officials. Many did their best to surrender their honors and sought refuge in the countryside, including in monasteries! Often, retreating from urban political responsibilities also meant abandoning commercial activities as well. In many parts of the Iberian Peninsula, farm lands within municipal jurisdictions were seized by powerful magnates.

Two important consequences flowed from the situation in Spain on the eve of the barbarian invasions, which eventually ended Roman control of the peninsula. The first was low productivity on the large estates, owing to the lack of interest on the part of the farm proletariat, combined with inefficient management. The other involved the intensification of authoritarian patterns implicit in the Roman social and governmental structure, a circumstance which continued throughout the subsequent Visigothic domination and which was reinforced in the Church's hierarchical system, both Arian and Catholic. It is probably not so difficult to understand why barbarians could enter Spain with relative ease. Probably the immense mass of peasantry felt they had nothing to lose by a change and certainly little incentive to fight for the preservation of a situation disastrous to their wellbeing. Nor for that matter was the large mass of Hispano-Romans either armed or trained for warfare.

This long association of the Visigoths with Rome in Dacia (roughly modern Rumania and adjacent areas), since the time of the Emperor Aurelian (270-275 A.D.), when he was forced to abandon that important province to the Goths, gradually resulted in the transformation of many of their original attitudes and internal structures. Among these was the evolution of an aristocratic landowning class positively influenced by the Roman example. When they entered southern Gaul, and later Spain, including through Catalonia, this characteristic was firmly established in the Visigothic political, military, and social culture.

41

In line with the Roman doctrine of ceding lands to settled allies, the Visigoths did the same as they pushed into southern Gaul, Catalonia, and into central Spain. Historical evidence suggests that the only people affected by this practice were important Galo-Roman landowners, when some of their possessions were sized by the new aristocratic military Visigothic class.[1] Despite the loss of lands, local magnates welcomed the new associations because the Visigoths imposed tranquility on the turbulent countryside, acting in the name of Rome and possessed of effective military means. Land areas owned by the Galo-Roman and Hispano-Roman aristocracies were so considerable that they could well afford to lose substantial holdings and still retain great wealth.

Visigothic Invasions

The invasion was a profound development in Iberian history, one which led to the reign of these new invaders that lasted 250 years. Their creation of a unified independent kingdom, coupled to their long tenure in the peninsula, meant their political and legal systems would seep into the life and culture of Catalonia and other parts of Spain, not to mention the emergence of the Kingdom of Asturia, which became an early spearhead of the Reconquest movement that led ultimately to the ouster from Spain of the Moslems some 700 years later.

Briefly put, in 376 under intense pressure from the Huns, the fierce and savage people from Central Asia, the Goths found themselves in an untenable position in Dacia and so sought Roman help. Roman officials saw the Goths as possible allies against the Huns and so permitted them to cross the Danube and settle within the Empire. All the Goths, some 200,000 men, women, and children, moved that year. Roman officials, however, proved abusive and did not live up to commitments made to them, which led the latter to rebel against Rome. The Goths were successful enough to lead to a friendly co-existence, but eventually they wanted to find land they could settle permanently. To make a long story short, tensions with the Romans sparked and in 410 the Goths sacked Rome and ravaged southern Italy. In 412 the Goths marched into southern Gaul, and in either 414 or 415 crossed Pyrenees, establishing their headquarters in

Barcelona. Their leader, Ataulf, sought to develop friendly relations with Rome and so concluded a pact with Emperor Honorius by which he agreed to return the Emperor's sister to him, Gala Placidia, who had been captured during the assault on Rome. The *quid pro quo* was Rome's consent to the settlement of the Visigoths in southern Gaul, in other words, also in what is present-day Catalonia.

The agreement collapsed, however, because Ataulf seized Narbonne, and married Gala Placidia, thereby thwarting the aspiration of Constantius, the highest ranking Roman military figure in Gaul who wanted her hand in marriage. Meanwhile Honorius was having difficulty retaining his throne, while Ataulf attempted unsuccessfully to seize Marseilles. Constantius pursued him back across the Pyrenees and set up his headquarters in Barcelona in 415. Ataulf's own people assassinated him, and his successor, Sigeric, was in turn assassinated a week later. The next Visigothic leader, Wallia stabilized the political situation by establishing relations with Honorius and returned to him his sister who then married Constantius. Meanwhile, the weakened Roman Empire was continuously invaded by Barbarians from northern Europe. In 406 Vandals, Alans, and Suevi crossed the frozen Rhine and swept through Gaul and, three years later, into Spain, where they began to settle.[2] Tarraconensis was spared. Wallia remained allied with Rome and so helped to fend off the new invaders into the Iberian peninsula and he controlled lands on both sides of the Pyrenees, even establishing a capital in Toulouse. Wallia proved successful in holding back the invaders in the areas he controlled. While the history of Roman-Vandal relations in the early 400s is rife with warfare, competition, and events occurring all over the peninsula, Roman legal, Church, and administrative practices perdured in northeastern Spain. The invaders were subsumed into the local cultures in Spain and eventually became Christians as well, certainly by the middle of the sixth century, they even having given up use of Germanic languages in favored of local Romanized idioms.[3]

The Visigothic presence in the peninsula is a dreary tale of regicides, rebellions, and continuation of social evils in the late Roman Empire, aggravated by economic stagnation. But for Spain their history proved crucial because it was during these years of a unified kingdom that the Arab invasion took place, made possible by the myriad of disloyalties, dynastic rivalries, and greed evident among the Visigoths when the Moslems came into Spain in the early 700s A.D.

However, the key point is that the Visigoths inherited and used Roman practices, thereby passing those on to subsequent kingdoms in Spain. As Catalan historian F. Soldevila noted, it was their "lengthy residence in southern Gaul" that made them so Romanized, mixing Germanic, Roman, and canonical elements. He argued that "the institution of monarchy, in its form, recalls the Roman model; the territorial division is recalled; in part in its Hispano-Roman municipal aspect with respect to the evolution and development of the Visigothic city and municipality," along with the administrative, fiscal, civil, military, and legal systems.[4] The majority lived in central Spain, suggesting that other parts remained largely Roman in their style of government and society, including Catalonia.[5]

Visigothic Legal Traditions

After the establishment of tenuous frontiers between al-Andalus (Arab name for Islamic Spain) and the Christian groups to the north in the early 700s A.D., it was a situation in which more than three quarters of Spain was in Moslem hands and obviously the Visigothic monarchy in disarray and disintegrated. There next emerged the substance for three Christian nations destined to serve as the beginnings of the effort to retake the peninsula from the Arabs, the Reconquest. All three differed from each other in considerable detail, especially in their origins and subsequent development, circumstances which over the centuries militated against the possibility of a groundswell for unification. These three were the Asturian-Leonese kingdom, Navarre, and the Catalan counties which in time came under the hegemony of the Counts of Barcelona, and discussed in the next chapter. The kingdoms of Aragon and Castile emerged somewhat later.

The emergence of a national concept under the Visigoths was essentially the creation of its monarchy, one resting on the will of the sovereign and supported by a small layering of Visigothic and Hispano-Roman aristocracy. There never existed a strong sentiment among the masses of non-Visigothic and nonaristocratic Hispano-Roman peoples in that direction. Hence, when the Christian kingdoms came into being, in general there existed a sense of regional identification and common religion, a feeling shared by local ruling elites. This sense of loyalty towards the *patria chica* (one's home town or area) is still evident in modern Spain. When, in time, peninsular unity once more was achieved it occurred by marriage at the apex of the monarchies through the union of Ferdinand and Isabel. But this only occurred after centuries of wrangling among the various ruling families, a key factor in the long drawn out nature of the Reconquest. Had the Moslems not been similarly plagued there probably would never have been a Reconquest.

Undoubtedly, with the disruption of the machinery of state in the nascent kingdoms and in the Carolingian marches in the eastern end of the Pyrenees, there was much improvement in the administrative structures of the new political entities. Nevertheless, despite the inevitable reliance on local custom and in the application of justice, institutions reflecting Roman origin, which were modified by the Visigoths, survived. The extent of this development varied in the different regions and resurfaced with surprising vigor once the new kingdoms and countships became firmly established. This development was particularly reflected in the legal systems when territorial law flourished anew.

Two reasons account largely for why much of the Visigothic order of political life with its Romanized underpinnings survived. The retreating Visigothic and Hispano-Roman aristocracy and high clergy, who sought refuge in the mountainous areas, brought with them their value systems and imposed these practices in regions coming under their control. Another factor was the later repopulation in Asturias and Leon, and to a lesser extent in Catalonia, by Arabized Christians (Mozarabs) who were eventually removed from Islamic lands in which they remained. They had preserved Visigothic law in effect at the time of the Islamic conquest for the administration of their own communities with the consent of the Arab conquerors.

Recall that after Alaric's defeat by the Franks at Vouillé in 507, Roman institutions in Hispania were largely in place, both in the northeast corner and in parts of central Spain, under the control of the Visigoths for about one hundred years. Most of the rest of Spain looked after itself. Another consideration stemmed from the circumstances that between Wallia's founding of the Visigothic kingdom based in Toulouse and Alaric's disaster, the Visigoths lived in the midst of an intensely Gallo-Roman atmosphere. This experience, which extended over ninety years, heightened keen awareness of Roman law and administrative systems. For a people who already were the most Latinized of the Germanic tribes before moving into southern France, and who had demonstrated ease in adapting to Roman ways, the task of a pragmatic approach to government proved no unsurmountable task.

In their kingdom in Toulouse, the invaders had established a dual legal system. The Gallo-Romans generally retained the laws in effect. Most administrative bureaucratic positions continued to be held by the later. The Visigoths initially functioned under their own laws after adjustment for circumstances of the conquest such as apportionment of lands. They kept the army and its command essentially as a Visigothic institution, and also the key responsibilities in government. After Vouillé the same approach was adopted in the establishment of the Kingdom of Toledo.

In reviewing briefly the evolution of the legal system in Visigothic Spain, we should also account for earlier developments in Toulouse. In 475 Euric, the reigning Visigothic monarch, introduced a new code associated with his name. Because of its antiquity, it was known as the *lex Antigua Visigothorum* (ancient law of the Visigoths). The code consisted generally of some 363 chapters written in Latin, divided into titled sections, much in line with Roman methodology for codification. In order to reconstruct missing sections, specialists achieved limited success through the study of laws governing the early Bavarians, which were based on Euric's Code.[6]

The *Liber iudiciorum*, a much later compilation developed in Spain long after the collapse of the Toulouse monarchy, also served as a source since it incorporated some of Euric's provisions. The *Liber* was initially undertaken at the quest of King Khindasvith (642-653) and finished by his son King Reccesvinth (653-672). The *Liber* was a most important work which influenced legal thinking beyond Spain well into the Middle Ages. In essence, it reconciled Visigothic and Roman law, thus ending the dual legal system. This measure, combined with the earlier conversion to Catholicism from Arianism of Recared (586-601), aided in the fusion of the Hispano-Roman peoples, a process interrupted by the Arab invasion of 711. The two developments proved far-reaching since they eliminated serious causes for dissensions between the two peoples. Without their removal the task of Reconquest would have been much more difficult or perhaps impossible.

Over time, these laws evolved. Principal among these was additional legislation under Euric's son, Alaric II (484-507). Variously referred to as *lex romana Visigothorum*, *lex Theodissi*, *Liber legume*, Breviary of Aniano, or more commonly as Breviary of Alaric, it applied mainly to Gallo-Romans. It was prepared in 506 based on extracts from the Theodosian Code (proclaimed in 438 by Emperor Theodosius II), grandson of Theodosius the Great, last emperor of a united Roman empire who left the eastern half to Honorius and the west to Arcadius, father of Theodosius II. It had provisions to cover aspects not included in Euric's Code.

Early Christian Legal Traditions

Parallel with Visigothic legal developments was the evolution of canonical law. These referred chiefly to church matters, but in Spain after Recared's conversion the church councils held in Toledo, they also reflected on occasion concern for matters of secular interest, particularly when prompted by the reigning monarch. Actions by councils relating to church matters resulted in the compilation in the sixth century of the *Collectio canonum Ecclesiae Hispana*, or simply *Collectio Hispana* (Collection of canons of the Spanish Church).

In Catalonia, where the Reconquest was spearheaded by the Carolingian Franks, there soon appeared the *capitularies*, ordinances decreed by the Carolingian monarch, their counts or delegates to the Spanish March, in the border areas between the southern frontiers of the Frankish kingdom and lands under Moslem control. These ordinances, regulations, or decrees reflected considerable Roman influence both in content and form. Nevertheless, remnants of the Gothic order survived. They were frequently taken into account in the *capitularies*, affecting zones under Carolingian influence which resulted from the movement into Frankish territory by Goths and Hispano-Romans fleeing from the Arab invaders.

Navarre and Aragon, situated between the two developing states on both ends of the Pyrenees, received legislative and administrative impulses from their neighbors, as well as from the north side of the Pyrenees, the result of transmontane royal marriages. But these outside influences proved minimal in comparison to the juridical evolution that stemmed from localized experiences.

The breakdown of Visigothic structural order led to an acceleration in the fusion of Goths and other races in the non-Moslem areas. The term *Hispani* even emerged as a designation for the people in the peninsula north of the Islamic territories. In the eighth and ninth centuries, the drive to the Christian kingdoms and countships in Catalonia was directed mainly at stemming the tide of Moslem encroachments. For generations their monarchs and counts were essentially military leaders whose primary energies were devoted to the requirements of defense, and only secondarily to matters concerning the organization of governments and the development of legal institutions. In general, the people who repopulated the frontier regions, whether as farmers or laborers in new urban clusters or agricultural estates, also served as soldiers called upon to defend their holdings or assist the kings and counts in military operations.

As Christian kingdoms came into being facing the Arabs, so too did the important institution and notion of *fueros*. These contained a listing of rights and obligations, and frequently details concerning the use of lands for agricultural and other uses. They were issued by kings and counts, and later by subordinates of each. These contained considerable provisions for self-government resting on a broad democratic basis, a circumstance which later led to serious conflicts when the monarchs encroached on and crimped these rights. In fact, the tendency of monarchs, prime ministers, and dictators to do this remained a problem down through the dictatorship of General Francisco Franco in the middle decades of the twentieth century. The long and important history of *fueros* need not detain us here; however, it is important to note that they also existed in Catalonia. There, the counterpart of *fueros* to some extent were the *consuetudines* or *costumes*. Legal evolution for cities and localities in Catalonia echoed closely the influences received from France, with the result that feudalism became firmly established in the region. It also may account for the reason why Catalans were in historical terms probably the most legally minded people in Spain.

Catalonia and the Start of the Reconquest

So, what we have described over the past many pages has been the legal and governmental administrative heritage of the Catalans and the other Christian kingdoms by the time the Arabs were occupying large swaths of Spain and even invading France through Catalonia. Little is known specifically, however, about what happened in Catalonia during the first fifty odd years of the Arab conquest. We know that during the first flush of the Arab sweep, the Moslem advance carried well into Septimania. Narbonne was strongly garrisoned and it was not until 751 that Pepin the Short recovered permanently the city and outlying areas. Barcelona, Gerona, and Lerida were in Arab hands during the first half century of Islamic control, as the Arabs secured the pathways for forays into southern France. In the Pyrenaic areas, save for those sectors affecting access to France, in all probability local chieftains were not interfered with by Islamic authorities so long as they paid their taxes and if they gave no comfort to the Franks from the north. Hence, a working arrangement appears to have existed between Arabs and indigenous leaders in the high eastern Pyrenees for their mutual benefit. Since Barcelona remained under Arab control until taken by Frankish troops in 801, the liberation of Catalonia did not commence until much later than that of the northwestern sections of Spain. When it did occur, the drive was essentially a Frankish effort, assisted to a much lesser degree by Goths and Hispano-Romans who had fled into Septimania and other areas in southern France. Furthermore, the Islamic occupation of Provence-Septmania did not end until 759. That of Aquitania occurred between 760 and 768, as a result of Pepin the Short's policies of bolstering the southern flank of his domains.

Unfortunately, neither Arab nor other sources indicate what happened to the considerable number of Hispano-Romans living in the lowlands and along the coastal areas of Catalonia. Did the majority flee, seeking refuge in the Pyrenees and France? Or, did most remain and convert to Islam? Alternatively, did they retain their Christian faith and way of life, coexisting with the conquerors and paying taxes levied on non-Moslems? That there existed depopulated lands in the countryside is unquestionable, as repopulation sparked by the Franks eventually took place and has been documented. But the question of numbers remaining is still unsolved, particularly with regard to cities and towns. The obvious importance of numbers of people of particular ethnic or social backgrounds is critical to any real understanding of those characteristics which carried forth from one generation to another, influencing political predispositions. In sorting through the period of early Arab presence, the impression is that we know more about the demographic composition of Spain during the Roman era. While there is much work yet to be done by historians and archaeologists, fortunately the political actions of a few people suggested patterns of behavior that could be attributed to the societies they represented. As with the actions at the time the Roman Empire declined and the Visigothic kingdom flourished, by looking at the Arab-Christian balance-of-power we find insights to augment meager data for the period.

Arab-Christian Balance-of-Power

The deeper one enters the period of the Reconquest, the more essential it is to understand Catalan activities within the broader context of Arab-Christian events.

Coinciding with the death of Alphonso I in 757, Arab leadership changed in Damascus and a new set of leaders ruled with Baghdad as their capital. One byproduct, however, was that a Umayyad prince escaped from Damascus, Abd al-Rahman, made his way to Spain, and reestablished his family dynasty in al-Andalus. There he established the Umayyad line of independent emirs, later called caliphs (756-929), who brought Islamic al-Andalus to extraordinary heights of achievements in such areas as science, medicine, and law, to a name a few.

With the advent of Abd al-Rahman I, the first phase of the Arab adventures in Spain, that of the appointed governors from Damascus (711-788) with their capital in Seville, was over. Abd Rahman (756-788) brought discipline and order to his new domain, stabilized the uneasy frontier to the north, blocked important Carolingian efforts to penetrate into Catalonia, and achieved notable economic successes. If Abd al-Rahman had not emerged on the scene and internecine squabbles among the Moslems continued, the total disintegration of the Arab effort could well have happened early. By the same token, the expansion of Alphonso's dominions from those in remote mountainous areas to a realm extending to Galicia and lands somewhat beyond the Cantabrian range and the regrouping of Christian forces, made possible by the disorders within al-Andalus during the emirate (governate) area, rendered out of the question any prospect for total Arab conquest of the peninsula. Furthermore, the presence in France of a strong military line of able monarchs, fully aware of the menace to the south, eliminated the possibility of any significant Islamic invasion of France.

Over many subsequent years the Christian kingdoms and countships grew slowly. But the tilt in the direction of an inevitable and unrelenting Christian drive against Islamic lands did not really become manifest, or actually occur, until the abolition of the evolved Umayyad Caliphate in 1031 and with the advent of Islamic "party Kings" in a thoroughly fragmented al-Andalus. But we are getting ahead of ourselves. With the beginning of the Umayyad dynasty with Abd al-Rahman in 756 and the death of Alphonso I in 757, the stage was set for completely new relations between the areas firmly under Christian control and al-Andalus. For the next 300 years profound changes developed in the two territories internally and in the contest for supremacy. The Christian kingdoms and countships consolidated their holdings and by the end of the tenth century had expanded deep into Islamic lands, particularly into Castile, despite occasional important upsets. Internally, a new order gradually came into being varying in the different regions as the result of circumstances. Nevertheless, whether in the Asturian-Leonese kingdom or Emerged Castile as an independent entity, or in French influenced Navarra, or in Catalonia where the anti-Islamic drive was spearheaded by the Franks, evidence of the Hispano-Visigothic heritage was discernable in varying degrees with respect to church, language, government, and law.

By the end of the eleventh century, to the modern historian, it would be clear that the inexorable Christian push would continue to its logical conclusion, despite grave internal dynastic changes and disturbances in both camps. Catalonia typified this pattern. However, the idea of Christian Reconquest was solidly a mystic objective from which there would be no turning back. It was now a question a time before the expulsion was completed.

CHAPTER FOUR
POLITICAL ORIGINS AND REGIONAL IDENTIFICATION IN NATION-BUILDING: THE CASE OF CATALONIA, 809-1035

Discussions about the political origins of nations are inextricably linked to regional identifications. Long before modern nation states were created, in region after region, groups of political elites, tribes, and communities competed for control of specific geographical footprints. Dynastic struggles and the role of local elites proved crucial in creating ever-larger political and social entities over time. As this study was being written, the process was again playing out in Iraq, where three different ethnic groups with long histories extending back long before European nations turned the entire region into a cacophony of colonies, were once again sorting through who should dominate specific parts of the area. The process was complicated by the fact that within each ethnic group were differing religious, tribal, and political groups competing for attention and political control. Africa continues to sort out tribal borders in the wake of freedom from European colonization. It is a long process of nation-building and in each case, was driven by dynastic or otherwise political and military initiatives that were complicated and took time to work out. It is an historic process that characterized the development of the modern nation state in Europe, for example. One of the most dramatic illustrations of that process at work is the case of Catalonia, located in the northeast corner of Spain, which in the process of acquiring a local national identity spent centuries in political and military rivalry. While tedious to document and describe that experience provides the political and social DNA strands that help define many of its modern features.

For that reason, the Catalan case is as urgent and instructive today as it has been for historians of modern European political affairs for centuries.

The question of how political and cultural differences developed between Catalonia and Castile is also one of the central issues in Spanish historiography. Today, as a thousand years ago, regionalism was and is a central concern in Spanish (Iberian) politics. The area is important too, occupying six percent of the Iberian landmass, serving as home for 6.4 million people (16 percent of modern day Spain's total population), not counting another quarter of a million residents in France, and historically a center of much Spanish economic activity. Today it is also one of seventeen autonomous regions within Spain. By any means chosen, Catalonia is important within the context of Iberian history. What one sees in the period down to the eleventh century is a differentiation already evident in attitudes toward law and government from other parts of Iberia, laying in place a pattern of differentiation that continues to this day. The reason for the evolution of cultural mores in Catalonia clearly different from those in other parts of Spain lies broadly in its historical roots, ethnic variation, and eventual outlook as a Mediterranean commercial people.

Finally, the story of Catalonia's political evolution in its early stages highlights the extensive integration of intra-dynastic politics across large swaths of Europe. It is easy to assume that due to poor travel conditions or primitive and slow means of communications that European regions operated in relative isolation. As the story told below makes abundantly clear, however, there existed much interaction among various polities across what is now modern day Germany, France, Italy, and Spain. The Catalan situation was thus a very international pan-proto-European case. Put in other terms, events in Catalonia affected the affairs of such far-away places as Bavaria in southern Germany, papal politics, and even the affairs of small kingdoms in northern France.

Specifically, the purpose of this study is to examine the political origins of Catalonia and more tactically, to explore how dynastic affairs of elite political groups brought about a distinction between the region and the rest of Spain. It is not a trivial or simple process. In the first place, it involved areas that we now call France, Germany, Spain, and Italy. For another, dynastic diplomacy in the early period studied in this monograph has not been well understood, particularly outside of a small circle of Catalan and European scholars. This circumstance is due largely to the complexity of the subject. For example, historians are faced with many counts and kings with the same name. Families intermarried, territories were exchanged with as little fanfare as one might trade in an old automobile for another or give a child a familial heirloom. A clearer explanation of what happened, despite the very limited amount of extant information available on this period, offers us the opportunity not only to understand Catalonia's origins but to contribute to a better appreciation of the importance such politics plays in the creation of a region distinct from its neighbors. It is in the caldron of such a process by which nations are created.

Such a review, when melded with the broad flow of historical events, can also help put into perspective the roles of individuals in affecting the destiny of nations. The merger of individual and collective historical events becomes important. For instance, the fact that the rollback of Islam was an extension of Carolingian policy at first, and later of Catalan counts with familial and deep cultural ties in former Septimania (roughly an area in southern France bounded by the Rhone River on the east, Uzes, Lodeve and Carcasonne to the north, Pyrenees and Mediterranean in its sourthern limits), was crucial to Catalonia's birth and origin. In contrast, Castile expanded southward as Galicians, Leonese, Navarrese, Asturians and other Cantabrian and Pyrenaic mountaineers melded together into early Castile, and pushed deep into Islamic territory as a result of their own efforts. A consequence was an inward looking Castile, introspective and military, individualistic, rural, frequently disdainful of commerce and industry for many centuries, and justifiably prideful of success in the eventual expulsion of Islam.[1]

To create a sufficient understanding of the process at work, and to illustrate its mechanisms requires that the specific dynastic rivalries and political events be described, to be sure, a tedious process. However, it is by looking at events at a level of detail normally not done, that we can reach conclusions with confidence about early nation-state building practices in Europe in general, and most specifically, in Catalonia and Spain.

Early Distinguishing Features of Catalonia

An important consequence of the different origins and evolution of these two states was, and is, the essentially European character of Catalonia in common with other nations and regions which formed part of the Carolingian empire. In contrast, Castile emerged quintessentially as an Iberian nation with *sui generis* traits setting it apart from continental Western Europe. While historians, Europeans, and Spaniards in general have argued over the question of Spain's Europeaness for centuries, replete with long dialogues over whether or not "Africa ends at the Pyrenees," the fact remains that there clearly were fundamental differences between Catalonia and Castile from very early times.[2]

Yet another characteristic of the region that derives from its early political construction concerns law and compromise. To one long associated with Catalonia and its way of life, there appears to stand out throughout the region's history a striking concern for proper observance of public and private law, amounting almost to an obsession. For a long time, Catalonia was the only region in Spain where a marked tendency to settle issues by compromise could be noted.[3] In other parts of Spain individualism generally led to a greater level of rigidity in holding views which, combined with a deep sense of personal honor, rendered "give and take" as a means for settling problems generally far more difficult. This pattern of behavior was still evident in the late twentieth century as in many earlier periods.[4]

The Catalan attitude towards law and to government was deeply rooted in its feudal experience which was equal to that of France and strengthened further by the growth of important and broadly-based classes of artisans and merchants, particularly in the port city of Barcelona. These elements saw in law and well organized government protection for the compliance of contracts and settlement of disputes. They gave rise to a substantial middle class which developed an effective parliament with the support of the Count of Barcelona, and later the kings of Aragon before the takeover by the Trastamaras.[5]

In contrast, within Castile no middle class emerged and feudal origins were most imperfect. Urban communities came to be ruled in the comparable period by oligarchies, even though these were for several centuries elected by the people. The "give and take" characteristic of a commercial society, such as that of Barcelona with its reasonable acceptance of compromise, was, for all practical purposes, absent in Castile. As the Christian conquest of Islamic-held Iberian lands moved southward, the Castilian culture went with it; one that reflected an authoritarian pattern. One has to conclude that this resulted in stagnation for centuries in the political evolution towards representative government.

Recall that Visigoths were the most Latinized of the barbarians who came under Roman sway. At the time of the Moslem invasion, Hispano-Romans and Visigoths in northeastern Spain, and in Septimania (which had come under control of the latter for some three hundred years until brought under the control of Charlemagne), molded a society largely the result of Latinized Visigothic concepts and structure. This phenomenon developed deeper roots in Septimania and Catalonia than in the rest of the Iberian Peninsula.[6] In fact, the Toledan dynasty faced separatist sentiments in the northeastern corner of Spain and in ancient Septimania, the latter which comprised a region of seven cities: Elna, Narbonne, Carcassone, Beziers, Agde, Magalone, and Nimes. If the Islamic invasion had not occurred, would Visigothic Toledo have prevented Catalonia and Septimania from evolving into an independent state? Thus, we need to acknowledge that the differences between the north-eastern corner of Spain and the central regions were apparent even in that remote period.

There are many vexing unanswered questions concerning the impact of the Islamic presence in Catalonia from the Llobregat River to Septimania. What proportion of the Hispano-Roman and Visigothic population remained or fled? How many embraced Islam? While Moslem control of Barcelona lasted about 85 years—a small interval when compared to the 800 years of Islamic presence in Iberia—the period of control, nevertheless, encompassed at least three generations, perhaps four, given the limited lifespan of the times. Much could have happened in terms of assimilation, depopulation, or repopulation by Moslem settlers.[7]

In all probability emigration into Septimania was considerable. The area was sparsely populated and Charlemagne welcome the émigrés by making land available to them while permitting Visigothic and Carolingian laws to function side-by-side, although

Church of Rome rituals were enforced to the detriment of Visigothic-Mozarab practices. Another reason to believe that Catalan areas were abandoned stems from the Carolingian policy of encouraging repopulation by returnees after the conquest of Barcelona by Louis the Pious. Interestingly, there does not appear to be much evidence indicating important movements of Mozarabs resettling in Carolingian Catalonia. Initially, the return of Catalonia to Christian control also was marked by tolerance of Visigothic laws and practices, although in time these blended with Frankish enactments and customs giving rise to distinctive Catalan jurisprudence (for example, the *Usatges de Barcelona* in 1058, 1060, 1068, and 1075).[8]

As occurred in other parts of northern Spain, and for that matter throughout medieval Europe, the eventual amalgamation of the early Catalan counties stemmed from family interrelationships, a process (or practice) which culminated in the union of Ferdinand and Isabel, that is to say, of the Crown of Castile with that of Aragon which included Catalonia.

Post-Charlemagnean Politics

Not long after Charlemagne's death in 814, internal dynastic conflicts erupted, which ultimately destroyed the unity of the empire. The problems stemmed from the marriage of Louis the Pious after the death of his wife to Judith, daughter of Count Welf of Bavaria, reputedly a beautiful, intelligent, and highly ambitious lady considerably younger than the emperor. From his first nuptials, Louis had three sons, a fact that complicated matters: Lothair, Pepin, and Louis. Then from his marriage with Judith came Charles.

After recovering from a serious illness, Louis considered succession issues before his second marriage. In 817 at the meeting of the imperial Diet (assembly) Louis dealt with the problem. Lothair would succeed as emperor inasmuch as he was the oldest son, and so was made co-regent and given the title of emperor in the plan. Pepin was granted governance of Aquitaine and Louis that of Bavaria, Bohemia, Carinthia, and certain Slavonic and Avar regions subject to the emperor. It was understood that Pepin and Louis would be subordinate to Lothair who, as part of the arrangement, was sent to govern Italy in 822. The *Ordinatio Imperaii* of 817 (as the agreement was known) also provided for a reduction in the size of Aquitaine, in that Septimania and the Spanish March were separated from the latter and transferred to Lothair's jurisdiction with the exception of Carcassonne.[9]

Consequently, the Duchy of Toulouse lost considerable territory with the creation of the Duchy or Marquisate of Gotia (Septimania and the Spanish March) which remained as a separate unit for about fifty years. Bera, a Goth, who was highly esteemed by the Carolingian dynasty and erstwhile Count of Barcelona, became the new Marquisate. Inasmuch as the population in Septimania was primarily Gothic in origin and that in the Spanish March lived largely in or near fortified castles in rather sparsely inhabited regions, the selection of Bera appeared as a logical move. Nevertheless, whether justified or not, in 820 Bera was removed from Gotia following charges of treason, and Rampon, Count of Gerona since 818, a Frank and vassal of Charlemagne, was appointed in his stead. The shift in command of so important a frontier post may not have been motivated by charges against Bera, who only suffered the loss of his Gotia responsibilities, but by imperial concern over Gothic disaffection and Bera's sympathetic governance of the region. Had he been guilty of treason, in all probability he would have been executed and his properties confiscated; neither happened.

Carolingian Frankish administrative, religious, political, and military policies were imposed in Septimania and the area immediately south of the Pyrenees. Local ethnic composition differed sufficiently from the rest of southern France to cause linguistic and attitudinal characteristics basic to and evident in present day Catalonia on both sides of the Pyrenees. All of these developments over time occurred despite the fact that for generations the French government had made it difficult for Catalan language, for instance, to perdue in its former Septimanian areas. Today, Catalan is still spoken by many families in the region, but solely because of speech at home since only French is used at school. In short, these earlier developments that took place during the Carolingian and Frankish eras were important to Catalonia's future development. To put yet a finer point on the issue, on both sides of the Pyrenees, including to the center and western ends, one is still struck forcibly by the endurance of the collective memories of people. To understand this point clearly, consider the case of Puerto Rico in the twentieth and twenty-first centuries. Close as it is politically, militarily, and culturally to the United States, and sharing the same sovereignty, yet after a century of association it retains in full flower its Hispanic traditions and language. The situation with respect to Catalonia vis-à-vis Madrid is not so different today, or even that of French Catalonia with regard to Paris, or perhaps that of French Canada and Ottawa.

It was against such various cultural and ethnic differences that dynastic politics continued in the northeastern corner of the Iberian Peninsula. It was an environment closely linked to events in other parts of Europe. Thus, for example, under intense pressure from Judith, at an assembly in Worms in 829 Louis altered the arrangement of 817 to benefit their young son, Charles. He was given a ducal title and assigned substantial lands in the Alsace region. Apparently at issue was a threat to the continued unity of the empire after Louis' death, as well as the ambitions of the three older brothers. Lothair, Pepin, and Louis (the son) and their partisans combined forces and at Campiegne in 830 took their father prisoner, who offered no resistance. Judith and her son Charles took refuge in a convent. The purpose of the revolt was to reinstitute the *Ordinatio* of 817, which the Emperor promised to respect. Pepin and his brother Louis, suspecting that Lothair planned to assume total power, shifted their support to favor the Emperor who regained the throne. By the fall of 831, Louis the Pious was totally rehabilitated. Through a new division of the empire Lothair gained Italy, while Pepin and Louis (son) were promised increased holdings. In order to satisfy Judith, who had rejoined her husband, Charles received all of Germany, most of Burgundy, Provence, Septimania, and other areas in central France. All these actions resulted in the annulment of the 817 agreement and an inevitable breakup of the empire.[10]

Unhappy with what they considered an excessive allotment of lands to Charles, Pepin, and Louis joined in a conspiracy to force a revision of the newest arrangement. In 832 Louis (son) attacked in Germany, but his father, with the support of loyal Saxons and other groups in the region, forced his submission. Louis (son) was arrested and his realm transferred to Charles the Bald, as

Judith's son is known in history. Pepin, unable to justify his subversive actions after personally approaching the Emperor, fled to Aquitaine and organized a force with which he forced his father to give way. By the end of the year all of southern France was in turmoil, which induced a general revolt in the empire. Once again the three older brothers combined their resources to revolt against the Emperor.

In 838 Pepin died and Aquitaine became the scene of civil war. One group supported the claim of Pepin II, his son, to the throne, while Louis the Pious and adherents pressed for Charles the Bald to succeed his half-brother to the Aquitanian throne. In light of the new circumstances arising from Pepin's death, Louis the Pious and Lothair met at Worms in 839. They agreed to a division of the empire between Lothair and Charles, with the exception of Bavaria which would remain with Louis.[11]

Lothair picked the area east of the Rhone—Saone and Meuse Rivers—and became emperor upon his father's death and protector of Charles. The latter received areas in France between the Meuse and Seine Rivers, parts of Burgundy, Provence, Neustria, Gascony, and Septimania, the Gascon, and the Spanish March. Within Aquitaine, Louis the Pious found it necessary to suppress anti-Charles revolts and was preparing to march against Louis who, unhappy with the Worms division, had invaded Germany, previously allotted to him, when the Emperor died on June 20, 839.

Strife among the three brothers and Pepin II immediately became the order of the day with varying fortunes of war until ultimately an agreement was reached in Verdun in August 843 with far-reaching effects on Europe. In essence, France and the Spanish March went to Charles the Bald and Germany to Louis. Lothair retained Italy and the title of emperor with only nominal acknowledgement by his brothers. The independence of the three states became a fact and the unity of the empire only a mirage.

Bernard of Septimania

How long Rampon served as Marquis or Duke of Septimania is unknown. But in 826, Bernard, one of the eight sons of Duke William of Toulouse, appeared as the Marquis of Septimania and Count of Barcelona. However, he arrived on the scene at the time of a serious revolt in the county of Barcelona and surrounding areas.

During Bernard's regime the Spanish March suffered internal disturbances as well as Moslem assaults. In his first tenure, when in 826 Bernard appeared on the scene as the Marquis of Septimania and Count of Barcelona, he faced a serious crisis. One Aizon, supposedly a native of the region (and whether Goth or Moslem uncertain), mobilized elements dissatisfied with the rapacity and harshness of Frankish rule and led a particularly damaging uprising. Aizon had been a prisoner at the Court of Aix-la-Chapelle, but had escaped and returned to the March. During the winter of 826-827 he ravaged the countryside, particularly in the area of Vich and Cerdanya. Aizon sent a brother to seek assistance from Abd al-Rahman II in Cordoba. The Emir responded by sending an important force under the command of Abu Marwan 'Ubayd Allah and together they laid siege to Barcelona in 828.[12]

Bernard requested help from the Emperor and Counts Matfred of Orleans and Hugo of Tours, both sympathetic to Lothair's cause. They marched with troops to assist Bernard. Whether because of personal enmity with Bernard, political reasons, or simply plain inefficiency, the relief force delayed along the way to the extent that Bernard was forced to rely on his own resources to beat off the siege. Unable to take the city, the Moslem army withdrew, marching to Gerona in an attempt to seize that metropolis. Failing also in this assault Abu Marwan had to be content with ravaging the general region over a period of some sixty days.

Abd al-Rahman's next attempt to take Barcelona came in 841 or 842 after the death of Louis the Pious; but the assault failed. The next effort came in 850, an initiative which met with no more success than the previous attacks. Archibald R. Lewis, a leading historian of early Catalan and southern French history, mentions the taking and sacking of Barcelona in 852 by a Moslem force, a circumstance not recorded, for example, by another distinguished expert on the period, E. Levi-Provençal.[13] Another historian, Ramon D'Abadal, examined in greater detail the matter of Islamic incursions in this period directed against the Spanish March, stressing the unusual fact that for the years between 828 and 842, both Moslem and Christian chroniclers were silent regarding raids across the frontiers by one or the other party.[14]

The period between 828 and 838 proved relatively tranquil in relations between Alfonso II of Asturias and Abd al-Rahman II. Likewise, Asturias and its expanded realm experienced few incursions during the reign of Ramiro I (842-850), Alfonso's successor, despite internal political instability. Problems within the emirate and Viking raids, and possibly personal military incompetence, may have accounted for Abd al-Rahman's lack of aggressiveness.[15] Whether there were two Islamic incursions or only one, and whether Barcelona was seized and looted as alleged by Frankish sources, is still not fully resolved. Historically, the significant reality was simply that Islamic invaders operated in the area, creating disruptions while giving focus to some of the politics of the region. Closer to the theme of our discussion, in the interim a truce was concluded between the Emir and Charles the Bald.[16]

For his efforts and success in saving the March, Bernard was promoted to the second most powerful post in the empire. He relinquished his responsibility as Marquis of Septimania, a position incompatible with his new appointment since the latter was essentially a military command. However, he did retain his *honores* as Count of Barcelona. He designated his brother, the Count of Rousillon, to function as viscount for Barcelona.

In 830 Louis the Pious prepared an expedition to suffocate an uprising in Brittany. Counts Hugo and Matfred were instructed to form a force to support Louis and Bernard who were on their way to the troubled zone. The three sons of the emperor who were unhappy with a change made in 829, which favored Charles, their half-brother, joined in a conspiracy to which Hugo and Matfred were participants. Instead of going to Brittany, their army marched on Paris. Louis, then king of Bavaria, and Pepin with an army from Aquitaine also marched with their forces to Paris. Isolated, Louis the Pious found it impossible to resist. Bernard fled to Barcelona, Judith and Charles took refuge in a convent, and Louis rode to Campiegne where he was forced to rescine the decisions of 829. A result of these events was the rise in influence of Hugo and Matfred who, unable to seize Bernard, took vengeance on his brother Heribert by blinding and then exiling him to Italy. Lothair gained the most from the successful conspiracy but excited envy and dissatisfaction in Pepin and Louis of Bavaria (or Louis the German as he is known in history). The result was a new conspiracy designed to restore their father's authority in order to counterbalance Lothair.

Three initiatives led to a new meeting of the Diet at Nymwegen in the fall of 830. There, Lothair proved unable to gain sufficient support. He asked for his father's pardon and was left only with Italian territory. In a new division of the empire the holdings of Pepin and Louis the German were increased. Charles was principally to receive Germany, Bergundy, Provence, and Septimania. While the formula would not long remain unchallenged, because of the extent of Charles' domains at the expense of his half-brothers, the disposition helped considerably in assuring the empire's breakup.

With the restoration of Louis the Pious' authority, Bernard of Septimania's fortunes once more turned for the better. He did not, however, regain his former high post in the court. Unhappy with this development, he returned to Barcelona and resumed governance also of the Marquisate of Gotia. Pepin and Louis the German, also dissatisfied with the recent arrangement in favor of Charles, in 831 formed a new conspiracy in which they were joined by Bernasrd. Louis with Bavarian forces entered Germany in 832, but the Emperor with the help of Saxons and other elements in the realm, forced him to submit. Pepin was fearful now of facing alone Louis the Pious and, therefore, attempted to needle his way back into his father's good graces by approaching the Emperor. Louis the Pious had him arrested and took away his possessions which were transferred to Charles.[17]

Because of his role in supporting Pepin, Bernard was removed from command of the Marquisate of Gotia and simultaneously lost his *honores* in Barcelona. Count Berenguer of Touloise replaced him. Additionally, Bernard's brother Gaucelm was removed his posts as Count of Rousillon and Gerona. But, both remained in the area of their former jurisdictions.

Pepin managed to escape from captivity, returning to Aquitaine where he assembled an army and confronted his father who, caught unprepared and with troubles spreading throughout the empire, had to give way. A consequence of Pepin's activities was that by the end of 832 all of southern France and the Spanish March was in a practical state of anarchy. Once more the three brothers, Pepin, Louis the German, and Lothair joined in a common effort to march against their father, the Emperor.

Matters became further complicated when Pope Gregory IV intervened in the conflict in the following year by accompanying Lothair across the Alps in his move to Alsace to join the other two royal conspirators. By early summer the two sides were confronting each other with the prospect of a major military showdown. But, negotiations to avoid bloodshed spread over several days, giving everyone time to reassess the circumstances. This delay, and the Pope's presence, had the unexpected result of the Emperor's abandonment by his leading supporters who switched to the brothers' cause. Three months later the Emperor was deposed at Campiegne, forced into a humilitating recital of alleged wrongdoings, and made to wear a penitent's attire. The Empress Judith was exiled to Italy and Charles packed off to confinement in a monastery. The Pope was aghast and deeply disturbed over events in which he had unwittingly played a part. Louis the Pious' inability (or unwillingness) to castigate his children, and weakness in resisting pressures from his second wife on behalf of Charles, had brought Charlemagne's magnificent inheritance to a low state. For the Pope the crisis meant a successful assault on paternal authority, a precedent from which his own institution could become vulnerable.[18]

As could be expected, elements favorable to the Emperor and shocked by the extent of his humiliations, took action to redress events. Lothair, who had held his father prisoner, resolutely fought off the latter's supporters, but for whatever reason and how, Louis the Pious managed to escape his captor. Rescued, he was restored to the imperial dignity in 834. He became reconciled with Pepin and Louis the German who feared Lothair's aspiration to assertion of unity in the imperial command. Louis the Pious thus found no alternative but to fight Lothair. At this point, Bernard of Septimania, always loyal to Pepin, was back in the Emperor's good graces. Once more he was reappointed to the Marquisate of Gotia command and presumably the countship of Barcelona.

In the course of the new struggle, Lothair seized Chalon-sur-Saone in Burgundy, a region pro-Emperor in its sentiments and in which resided Gaucelm, Bernard's brother and former, or perhaps reappointed, Count of Rousillon. Their sister Gerberga became a nun. In his hatred of Bernard, Lothair had Gaucelm executed and the nun tussled into a barrel and tossed into the Saone River where she drowned. Lothair, finding it impossible to destroy the coalition formed against him, abandoned the struggle and in 834 returned to Italy.

Recall that Berenguer of Toulouse had been given the Marquisate of Gotia and he was not of a temper to cede this important plum to the newly reappointed Bernard. Given the weakened power of the Emperor to impose his will on recalcitrant nobles, a conflict between Berenguer and Bernard appeared inevitable. However, Berenguer's death in 835 averted this prospect, and unchallenged Bernard acquired additionally the countship of Gerona and probably his late brother's *honores* in Rousillon.

Historians all make references to the extraordinary event which occurred at Strassburg, where Louis in the German language and Charles in Romance (or early French) swore perpetual alliance in front of their troops.[19] At a meeting in Verdun the brothers agreed that Louis would retain Germany, Charles the Bald to have France and Lothair would retain Italy, the title of emperor, and a narrow bit of territory from the Meuse to the Rhine, and from the Saone and the Rhone to the Alps (Belgium, Lorraine, the country of Burgundy, Dauphiny and Prevence). Historically, for the first time since the conquest of Gaul by Rome, the Rhine ceased to be the dividing line between Gallia and Alemania. In effect, Charles the Bald became the first king of France, Louis that of Germany, while Lothair continued as the one for Italy. At that crucial moment in European history Septimania and the Spanish March emerged as integral parts of the kingdom of Charles the Bald, that is, of France.

To return to Bernard, after Berenguer's death he seized Toulouse, apparently with impunity. With Septimania and the Spanish March under his control, Bernard was a power to be reckoned with. But he faced a serious dilemma. His friendship with Pepin I dated from the time of the latter's second rebellion against his father, a relationship which Bernard extended to Pepin II. On the other hand, Bernard and his relatives held important properties in Burgundy, an area loyal to Charles the Bald through his mother's family. A misstep could cost his Toulouse if he fell out with Pepin II. A similar error would most certainly involve loss of the properties in Bergundy should he offend Charles. Yet the conflict between Pepin II and Charles the Bald was irreconcilable. The problem was further aggravated by Bernard's deep hatred of Lothair, because of the execution of his brother, murder of Gerberga, and by the fact of Pepin II's support of Lothair.

In the face of these complex circumstances, Bernard adopted a policy of ambiguity. It was in his best interests to have Pepin II and his uncle Charles the Bald work out some *modus operandi*. He sought to do so and Charles, aware of his longstanding connection with Pepin II and his family, put him to the test. He acquiesced to Bernard's plan to meet with Pepin in the hope that an agreement could be reached. Bernard implemented this initiative without success and possibly without intending for his own personal submission to Charles. The final crisis for Bernard came when, after the Treaty of Verdun, where Pepin II had been excluded from any spoils, the latter decided to fight for his right to Aquitaine. In this situation Bernard was one of his supporters. In 844 Charles marched on Toulouse, seized Bernard, tried him for treason, and beheaded him.[20]

For the Marquisate of Gotia (Septimania and the Spanish March), Charles appointed Sunifred, Count of Urgel. Sunifred was possibly a Goth and certainly a native of the region related to the House of Carcassonne, who probably also received the countship of Barcelona. A wise and able administrator, Sunifred governed quietly from 844 until his death around 848.

Frankish Counts: Aleran, Udalric and Hunfrid

The able Sunifred was succeeded by Aleran, Count of Troyes, a Frank from the northern part of France who was alien to the ways of Septimania and the Spanish March, governing between 848 and probably 852. Circumstances surrounding his disappearance from the chronicles are murky, although he may have been killed in the defense of Barcelona. During his tenure an important rebellion was sparked by William, Bernard of Septimania's son, who continued his father's policy of siding with Pepin II, hopeful of recovering the Marquisate. Whether as a result of coordination or by coincidence, William's actions occurred at the same time as that of a similar movement organized by Count Sancho Sanchez, a Basque, who wanted to eliminate Frankish sovereignty in Gascony. In 847 severe Viking raids had ravaged the Bordeaux area, including the city itself, despite energetic efforts by Charles to defend the region. Sancho Sanchez launched his initiative, seeking to take advantage of Charles' embarrassment.

Through guile rather than force of arms, William seized Ampurias and Barcelona. Charles responded by meeting with Aleran at Narbonne to adopt counter measures. In the interim, Aquitaine was aflame once again with civil war and in the Spanish March turmoil intensified, stemming from William's subversion. At the beginning of 850 Aleran fell into a trap and was captured by William. But, in the same year, the Carolingian command, also through guile, seized William and executed him. With his death, the rebellion collapsed.

Another Frank, Udalric, Count of Narbonne, who probably also assumed the *honores* for Barcelona, followed Aleran. He assumed responsibilities for the Marquisate sometime between 852 and 854 and ruled until about 857. Little is known about events in the Spanish March during his tenure in office. However, it appears that Udalric participated in the great conspiracy of the nobles of the realm against Charles; in fact, his brother was one of the emissaries who approached Louis the German for that purpose in 858. Even though later reconciled with Charles, the defection presumably accounted for his removal from office.[21]

Udalric's successor to the Marquisate was another Frank and relative, Hunfred. Either towards the end of Udalric's term or the start of Hunfred's, the Spanish March had become the target of yet more Islamic action. Musa ibn Musa, then governor of Zaragoza, seized Tarrega on the boundary region of the county of Barcelona, simply adding to the political and military turmoil in the region.[22]

Hunfred, although initially a supporter of Charles in one of the latter's critical moments, rebelled in 863. He assaulted Toulouse whose Count Ramón died in the attack and declared himself Count of Toulouse, in effect reconstituting the domain which included Septimania and the Spanish March. But chaotic events within France, and Aquitaine in particular, in 864 led to a situation believed by Hunfred to be untenable and so fled to his estates in Italy. In an effort to clip Count Hunfred's wings and weaken his control over the vast area under his personal rule, as well as to marshal elements hostile to him, Charles established a new organization for the region on April 22, 865 while at the Diet then meeting at Servais. A reorganized Marquisate of Gotia included the counties of Carcassonne, Razes, and the northern sector with its capital at Narbonne. The Spanish March incorporated Confluent, Rousillon, and Cerdenya, with its capital at Barcelona.

Early in Count Hunfred's governance, Charles had concluded a peace treaty with Muhammad I which was to last for some thirty years. Hence, Charles hoped that the changes in the region and amicable relations with the Moslems would permit him greater leeway in dealing with problems elsewhere in the realm. One important result of the long period of peace was an extensive expansion of trade between Andalusia and Narbonne from which goods and slaves were further distributed northward. Most of this trade was in the hands of Jewish merchants who were protected in their enterprises. Products from the Far East and those of Western Europe were channeled into this trade. To the Spanish March came goods and slaves from Zaragoza to Lerida through Barcelona and Gerona and hence to Narbonne.[23]

In the new arrangement, a Frank, Count Saloman of Urgel-Confluent-Cerdanya, appears to have been appointed commander of the Spanish March. One expert, however, stresses that he was not the Count of Barcelona.[24] The other Frankish count appointed to Narbonne as Marquis was also named Count of Barcelona, Gerona, and Rousillon. This Bernard, referred historically as Bernard of Gotia (to avoid confusion with other Bernards concerned at one time or another with the region), was the son of Bernard, Count of Poitiers and grandson of another magnate who also held the same *honores*. His mother was a sister of the Count of Maine. Hence, he was alien to the region's predominant families. Yet, he had other *honores* in France and figured as one of the powerful magnates of the realm.

Saloman was a personality wrapped in legend. Very little in the way of hard facts are known about him. He could have been a Goth or a Frank, or be related to indigenous families; nothing is known for certain. There are some old ballads which are based on the story that he had participated in the assassination of Sunifred and that the latter's son, Guifred the Hairy, under fabulous circumstances, avenged his father by killing Saloman. But there is no hard evidence that such was the case. That he existed is fact, and that he was the last commander of the Spanish March appointed by the Carolingian dynasty is also true. Likewise, there is no doubt that in about 870, after the death of Saloman, Guifred the Hairy received these counties and ruled probably in conjunction with his brother Miró. That Guifred and his brother (or brothers) took advantage of the internal situation in France and political power plays between the House of Carcassonne and Toulouse to seize power, was not only possible, but probable. Guifred is universally accepted as the founder of the Catalan dynasty of Barcelona counts de facto independent of the Carolingian crown.[25] Recall that it was within the same time frame (about 872) that Raymond I seized the Ribagorza and Pallars, proclaiming himself count of the two regions.[26]

Independent Counts of Barcelona

When one thinks of early rulers of Barcelona, the counts of Barcelona come quickly to mind. But, as we have demonstrated above, local political leadership unique to what later would be called Catalonia preceded the counts of Barcelona by generations. Moreover, they were linked closely to monarchies and varies other political elites ranging from those in southern France to German territories, and had connections to Italian states. These interconnections were cosmopolitan, complex, and diverse, contradicting any notion that Pyrenaic or Catalan politics of the early Middle Ages were remote or of some "backwater" importance.

From the time of Guifred's rule to the death of Martin the Humanist, King of Aragon and Count of Barcelona, in 1410 the dynasty of the House of Barcelona governed Catalonia. The linkage with the adjoining kingdom came through the marriage of Ramón Berenguer IV of Barcelona and Petronila of Aragon in 1137. The origins of the House of Barcelona are not crystal clear, but it appears to have been closely related to that of Carcassonne. This probability has long been a matter of conjecture and debate. However, Catalan historian Ramón D'Abadal has come closest to settling the question. He forecefully and convincingly maintains that Count Bellon of Carcassonne and proprietor also of lands in

Confluent (area in France between Roussillon on the east and Cerdanya on the west bordering the Pyrenees on the south) was the father of Gisclafred and Oliba I, successive counts of Carcassonne; of Sunifred I, Marquis of Gotia, Count of Urgel-Cerdanya, Barcelona, Gerona, and Narbonne; and Sunyer I, Count of Ampúrias and Rousillon.[27]

Carcassonne continued in Oliba's family through his sons Oliba II and Acfred (also of Razes). A third son was an abbot in the region. Gisclafred left no male heirs. Sunifred I had four sons: Guifred the Hairy, who was the founder of the Barcelona dynasty; Miró I, Count of Confluent, Rouisson; Radulf, Count of Besalú; Sunifred, who was the Abbot of Arles. His brother, Sunyer I, had two sons: Dela and Sunyer II; both succeeded as joint counts of Ampúrias and Roussillon.

With so many names and people, it should be of little surprise that historians argued over the genealogy. The fuzzy quality and paucity of archivally-based evidence compounds problems for modern historians. Lewis, for example, does not concur with D'Abadal's assertion of Sunifred I's immediate descent from Count Bellon. He argued that it is "more probable that he was descended from Count Borrell of Ausona (Vich)."[28] However, Lewis does not question a family relationship between Sunifred I's and the House of Carcassonne, whatever that may have been. The fact remains that by 878 most of Septimania and the Spanish March were governed by closely linked family-interrelated counts, enjoying hereditary rights. In time Guifred the Hairy's descendents controlled the area as counts of Barcelona and eventually became kings of Aragon.

Related to developments in the Spanish March was the unfolding drama of the disintegration of the Carolingian holdings. In response to a plea from the Pope for assistance in warding off threats from Moslems and from northern Italian magnates, Charles the Bald sought to assemble an army to assist the pontiff who had fled from Italy to Provence in hopes of obtaining aid. Charles' efforts to form any army capable of embarking on the Italian adventure met with considerable difficulty. The high ranking nobles were far more interested in developing events at home and at best sent only their sons. A threat evolved with Carloman of Bavaria raising an army to challenge the newly designated emperor. Charles appealed to his vassals in France for reinforcements. Instead, he faced a rebellion and among the leaders included his brother-in-law, Boson of Provence and Lombardy, Count Bernard (Plantevelue) of Toulouse, and Count Bernard of Gotia. The rebellion affected the destiny of the House of Carcassonne and that of Guifred the Hairy. In essence, the counts of Carcassonne and Sunifred's sons remained faithful to the reigning French dynasty while Bernard of Gotia picked the losing side. This led to the legitimacy of the *honores* being seized by Guifred and his brothers (which belonged to Bernard of Gotia) and to the consolidation of the position acquired in Carcassonne by his relatives in their political tilting with Bernard Plantevelue.[29]

Charles died while en route to Italy in 877. Louis the Stammerer (877-879) succeeded his father as king of France. To secure support from the magnates he followed Charles' policy of granting domains still in his possession, a practice continued by his two sons, Louis III (879-882) and Carloman (879-884). These two brothers ruled without conflict between them, Louis III in Neustria and Carloman in Aquitania and Burgundy. But the disintegration continued. Provence became an independent kingdom and Lorraine was lost to Germany. Upon their accidental deaths, there remained a brother, Charles the Simple, posthumous son of Louis the Stammerer, but, who because of his youth, the nobles rejected in favor of Charles the Fat (832-888), third son of Louis the German. He had inherited Swabia from his father. When his brother Carloman of Bavaria died he found himself king of Italy in 880 and was crowned emperor of the Romans in the following year. When his brother Louis of Saxony died in 882 he acquired control over all of Germany and as a result of the French nobles' option in 885, after Carloman's death in 884, added the crown of France to his collection. Utterly inept, given to gluttony and pleasure, ruler by the accidents of fate of a reconstituted Charlemagnian empire, he was summarily deposed in 887 and died in a monastery or convent in 888.[30]

With the elimination of Charles the Fat, the empire's disintegration was complete. It broke apart into eight kingdoms: France, Navarre, Cisjurane, Burgundy, Transjurane Burgundy, Lorraine, Italy, and Germany. Through a policy of grants to nobles in exchange for their support, the heirs of Charlemagne had so reduced their resources that they were in no position—

even assuming personal ability—to fight off ambitious and powerful nobles. By the time of Louis the Stammerer, the king of France had practically no governmental authority and so chaos reigned throughout the realm. For the Spanish March the weakened state of the various kingdoms meant that survival and order fell to Guifred the Hairy and his relatives to provide. They rose to the responsibility required by these circumstances, but their actions also signified de facto independence from the French crown.

Yet, the connection with the French was far from interrupted. There remained *de jure* linkages as vassals of the French monarch, which were not severed until the thirteenth century. That meant events north of the Pyrenees would continue to influence those in Catalonia.

The Carolingians were German-speaking monarchs and viewed the emperor as head of the family, as evidenced by the elevation of the inept Charles the Fat to that post. However, the latter's inability to defend France against devastating raids by the Vikings or Norsemen, combined with resentment by French nobles against the Germanic cast of the Carolingians, led to the selection of Eudes (Odo), Count of Paris, who, because of a stout defense of Paris against the Vikings, received the Duchy of France, as king of France. Eudes (887-898) thus became the harbinger of the Capetian line of French monarchs. But, it is important to note that his governance extended only over lands between the Loire and the Meuse. He failed to break the independence of the southern sections of France, continued to face Viking assaults and was forced to deal with attempts by pro-Carolingian magnates to bring to the throne Charles the Simple, posthumous son of Louis II. Despite support of his relative, Arnulf, king of Germany, Charles' cause failed.

In the main, the purpose of the peers of the realm was not ardent support for a Carolingian monarch, but a means by which a weak and ineffectual king could sit on the throne, allowing them to do as they pleased.[31] Although Eudes could not extend his rule over Aquitaine, he did manage to force the Duke of Aquitania to forego the claim to title of king and to swear fealty to him. This proved to be a significant accomplishment because on Eudes' death, his brother Robert inherited the Duchy of France, while Charles the Simple became king of France without opposition and with nominal adherence of Aquitaine. It was Charles the Simple who gave the Vikings' chieftain, Rollo, lands which became Normandy, a move which resulted in the transformation of these Norsemen into Frenchmen.

Charles the Simple (898-922) was deposed and Robert, duke of France, elected king. In the civil war which ensued, Robert was killed in 923 and Robert's brother-in-law, Rodolph (Duke of Burgundy between 923 and 926), succeeded.

Hugh the Great, Duke of France, and brother-in-law of the deceased Robert, engineered the return to France from England where he had sought refuge, of Louis IV d'Outre-Mer (936-954). Louis IV was the fifteen year old son and heir of Charles the Simple. Bringing the boy back was a move designed to stabilize the highly chaotic conditions prevalent in France following Rodolph's death. Supported by nobles wary of High's power, Louis eventually attempted to seize full control of the situation. Hugh and his vassals and allies responded rapidly, imprisoned him for a year, and did not release the royal captive until Louis had agree to cede Laon to Hugh, the last asset of this kind owned by Louis. Louis appealed to the Pope and Otto the Great of Germany. Hugh was unawed by the Pope's excommunication, nor by Otto's might. Shortly thereafter, while hunting, Louis was accidentally killed.

Louis IV was married Gerberge, sister of Otto the Great of Germany. They had two sons, Lothair and Charles. Gerberga knew that without Hugh's help neither of her two minor sons could reach the throne, and thus sought and obtained his assistance. With Hugh as protector, the nobles accepted Lothair as king in 954. His proved to be a fearfully turbulent reign caused by the internal jockeying of France's magnates and the ambitions of Otto for Lorraine. Nevertheless, Louis IV sat on his throne for thirty-three years and died from natural causes. He was succeeded by his son, Louis V, who a year later (987) died from a fall off a horse. With his death, the Carolingian line of French kings ended.[32]

After Lothair's death, the great nobles of France met at Senlis to determine the succession. Lothair's brother, Charles of Lorraine, was a possible candidate. But apart from lack of resources with which to make good any aspirations to the throne, the fact that in order to hold the Duchy of Lorraine (Brabant) he had to swear fealty to the German monarch, posed a circumstance utterly unacceptable to the high French nobility.

Hugh Capet, son of Hugh the Great, Duke of France, Count of Paris and Orleans, abbot of three of the wealthiest abbeys in France, and as strong and powerful as any other peer in the realm, assumed became king and was crowned at Noyon. He reigned from 887 to 996, and his son Robert followed from 996 to 1031. The dynasty held the throne until 1108. However, it can be said that the first four Capetians reigned but did not govern. There was a long way to go before the powerful magnates could be obedient to a strong central monarch. The consequence for the Catalan counts of the chaos prevalent in France (particularly for the House of Barcelona) was to distance itself further from the French crown. That process, in turn, led to a more independent Catalonia over time, an area with strong cultural and political similarities obviously to areas immediately north of the Pyrenees but which began developing its own identity in the later Middle Ages.[33] A modern analogy of the process might be Canada and the United States. Both were born of a single Anglo-Saxon rule (English government) and culture, yet matured in nationhood as two separate political entities with similar but distinct cultural characteristics from both each other and their mother country, England.

Guifred (Wilfred) the Hairy and the Origins of a Catalan Dynasty

Louis II (the Stammerer) had succeeded Charles the Bald in 877, crowned at Rheims as "King of the French" and reconsecrated the following year at Troyes with Pope John VIII in attendance. He died in 879 after only some eighteen months on the throne. Events at Troyes proved crucial to the future of Guifred he Hairy, his brother Miró and Guifred's heirs. As occurred in the early history of Navarre and the Pyrenaic counties, the beginnings of the ruling dynasty in Catalonia is also obscure, owing to the lack of documentation, but not for the lack of effort, because for about the last century Catalan scholars have attempted to sort out fact from legend.[34] That he and his brothers existed and played key roles in the Spanish March is beyond a doubt as attested by church documents involving donations of land to support newly created monasteries. Remaining questions revolve mostly about the specifics of by whom, when, and how the various dignities were acquired. The only extant narrative for the period is the *Gesta Comitum Barcinonensium*, written in the twelfth century by monks in the monastery of Santa María de Ripoll in the province of modern Gerona. While the *Gesta* includes reflections of legends concerning Guifred's entry into Catalan history, these contain a core of substance. In general, the narrative contains considerable historical validity.[35]

In recent years, D'Abadal, more than any other scholar, has pursued intensively the issue of the first counts of Barcelona and his work may well be regarded as the most fruitful concerning the subject.[36] He conjectures, based on extensive research, that at the Council of Troyes, following a banquet given by Boson of Province in honor of Louis II, that Guifred was officially named Count of Barcelona, and possibly of Gerona as well, and that his brother Miró was named Count of Roussillon. A passing reference to Guifred and to his position in Barcelona in an Arab chronicle further confirms from a non-Christian source the fact of his status in the region.[37] The possession of Rousillon by Miró is based on firmer evidence.[38] In all probability Louis II merely confirmed officially what his loyal subjects, Guifred and Miró, had already seized by force of arms with the blessings of friendly churchmen resentful of the Metropolitan at Narbonne, under whose jurisdiction fell the sees in the Spanish March. It is significant that Guifred and Miró certainly sought to legitimize their actions by obtaining royal sanction. It is also extraordinarily important for Catalan political history to note that though the Troyes' designations were related to functional responsibilities, the chaos in France following Louis' death permitted the transformation of these *honores* into hereditary rights.

The long era of peace, which had characterized relations between the Spanish March and Islam, ended once Guifred was firmly in control of Barcelona. Mainly through inheritance Guifred had gradually acquired in addition to his original *honores* in Urgel and Cerdanya, the counties of Besalu (south of Rousillon and north of Gerona) and Confluent. With the addition of the counties of Gerona and Barcelona, he acquired possession of contiguous territory ranging along the Pyrenees (including Andorra) and somewhat southward from roughly the Segre River to the Mediterranean and along the coastline. But the center of the region consisted of the former county of Ausona (Vich), which had suffered acute devastation at the time of Aizon's rebellion in 826-827, and had remained mostly or entirely depopulated. This no-man's land of a situation contributed to containing the conflict to a minimum between the counts of the Spanish March and the Banu Qasi in the region of Lerida.

For a capable military strategist and ambitious statesman of Guifred's caliber, the need to fill in the center proved essential for the defense o the coastal counties. He, thus, embarked on an important policy of repopulation; one, which in time, inevitably led to clashes with the Bani Qasi. Recall that about that period Alfonso III of Asturias (866-911) had systematically expanded his frontier, leading to endemic warfare with Cordoba. Guifred's intent to expand similarly toward the west, posing a threat to Lerida, was not lost on the Banu Qasi. The demographic growth which made it possible for Alfonso III to broaden his realm through populating abandoned or sparsely inhabited areas also held for the eastern end of the Pyrenees. The combination of surplus manpower in Guifred's Pyrenaic holdings and refugees who had fled into the mountains of central Old Catalonia at the time of Aizon would provide the nucleus for a repopulation drive.[39]

There is no evidence on how great a demographic transfer took place; probably not more than several thousand people, judging from indirect references to the smallness of settlements, particularly where these were initiated or implemented by churchmen. But, the outcome of Guifred's efforts was a surprising number of settlements in the present districts of Berga, Ripoll, the plain of Vich, that of Bages, of which modern Manresa is the principal city, and as far westward as Cardona after crossing the Llobregat River.[40] So notable was Guifred's success that apparently with royal assent, or possibly without it, he could add to his dignities that of Count of Ausona. The revitalized county not only signified an important economic asset, because of the fertility of the areas reclaimed, but also established a defensive system to the west of his holdings. Guifred's expansion appears to have extended as far southward as the Montserrat region. And, in fact, he lent support to the founding of the famous monastery of that name, probably with monks from Ripoll.

Guifred followed roughly the same policies in his effort at repopulation as those of his peers in Asturias, Leon, Castile, and Navarre. In the establishment of Cardona for military and economic purposes, the charter granted this community was designed to stimulate immigration and resembled some of those characteristic of Castilian expansion.[41] Acquisition of land by immigrants after use for a certain number of years (*Aprisio*) was not too dissimilar and also had a similar result, that is to say, the creation of numerous small independent farms. In time, ownership of these small farms became a distinctive economic, political, and cultural characteristic of the Catalan region of Spain.

Foundation of churches and monasteries through Guifred's direct efforts and encouragement (as well as by private interests) likewise played an important role in the repopulation drive. Monasteries which acquired great reputations during the Middle Ages founded by Guifred and his wife Winidild included San Juan de las Abadesas and Santa María de Ripoll. These and others established by him reflected the influence and rites of the Church of Rome as did those in France.

But his reign ended when, in one of the many conflicts with Moslem neighbors, according to an Arab source, Guifred suffered a mortal wound at the personal hands of the Banu Qasi chieftain, Lope ibn Muhammad ibn Lope, in the storming of a castle in 898 near Barcelona.[42]

Guifred's Contributions

Guifred's importance in early Catalan history warrants further analysis. Early in his career he managed relations with France with the utmost tact, because without Carolingian cooperation his ability to expand against Moslem-held lands might have taken a different turn. Documents from Guifred's era reflect that after a prudent wait he acknowledged Eudes' position as Charles the Fat's successor and later Charles the Simple. But, Guifred's behavior during the troubled times in France when he recognized monarchs who were in no position to assist in fending off the Bani Qasi or in the repopulation initiative, offers interesting points for speculation. There is no indication that he at any time sought to convert the Spanish March into a kingdom with himself as monarch. Yet it was a period when kingdoms were sprouting in Spain and France. The fact that Guifred did not transform the marquisate or county under his control probably accounts for why Catalonia never became a monarchy, even when it eventually had all the attributes necessary to be one and despite the fact that its count of Barcelona was regarded as an equal by Spanish monarchs.

Admittedly, Guifred's energies were consumed in expanding and consolidating his realm and in defense against the Moslems. The process proved slow, time consuming, and expensive. He may have felt insufficiently strong enough to assert de facto independence by a formal break with the French crown. Astute politician that he was, he knew how rapidly political and military fortunes could change. That Eudes could have mobilized sufficient muscle to break a Spanish March rebellion would have been a possibility. And it was only a short time after Charles the Simple ascended the throne that Guifred met his death. Perhaps if he had lived long enough and fully consolidated his holdings, Guifred's aspirations might have changed. That he was a prudent ruler is apparent by remaining neutral in the civil war between Eudes and Charles the Simple in 893.

There were, furthermore, other considerations pertinent to the times. Three factors could have influenced Guifred's attitude towards a reigning French monarch. His original designation was that of an official, but he was also bound by an oath of allegiance as vassal (*fideles*) and was proprietor by inheritance of lands in the region under his mandate. That he and his immediate successors were keen about assuring the legitimacy of their *honores* and its legal implications is clear. In establishing monasteries, churches, and other institutions, he invoked the name of the French monarch in some fashion. He sought royal sanction for precepts affecting not only lay matters but also those of the Catholic Church and cooperated with prelates in this respect. Perhaps he believed that if, in an era when vassalage had become an important basic element in the social and political structure, he ignored its implications that the many levels of society below him might feel free to do likewise.

In addition, he could not ignore the possible reactions of his relative, Sunyer II, Count of Ampúrias, who had inherited responsibilities from his father, Sunyer I, Guifred's uncle. Sunyer II was a doughty warrior and seaman who had not hesitated to raid the Moslem coasts. But underlying these many aspects, the fact remained that Guifred apparently sought to cloak his activities under a mantle of royal legitimacy, a characteristic of the House of Carcassonne and that of Barcelona. Perhaps this early preoccupation with the consequences of law contributed or initiated traditional Catalan regard for loyalty as a characteristic of national behavior.

Guifred's Successors

Guifred I and Winidild had nine children, five boys and four girls. He divided the counties among his heirs as follows: Guifred II, also known as Guifred Borrell, received Barcelona, Ausona, and Gerona with his brother Sunyer functioning as a participant in their governance with the title of count; Miró acquired Cerdanya-Confluent and Besalú; Urgel went to Sunifred; while Radolph (Randolph or Rodulph) became abbot of Santa María de Ripoll. Emma became abbess of San Juan de las Abadesas. Her sisters Quixilo, Riquilda, and Ermesind presumably married regional counts, thus, extending family interrelationships. Recall that Count Miró (referred to in history as Miró II or the Younger) married Ava, sister of Count Raymond II of Ribagorza. Guifred's brother Miró is known as the "Elder" to avoid confusion between the two Mirós.

Guifred II (898-911) followed generally his father's prudent policies. He continued to strengthen the frontiers, supported monasteries established by Guifred I, as well as the newly founded San Cugat del Valles. Acknowledgement of Charles the Simple as king and lord was evident in obtaining royal approval for the purchase of lands in the county of Ampúrias. He is believed to have been married to Garsenda, daughter of a prominent family in Rousillon. Guifred II left no male heir and his brother, Sunyer, ruled as Count of Barcelona, Ausona, and Gerona until 947 when he abdicated and embraced monastic life until his death in 950.

Between 898, when Guifred II succeeded his father, the later succession of Sunyer, until the latter's abdication in 947 and death in 950, there appears to have been little violence on the frontiers with Islam. Extant Arab and Christian chronicles reflect little information on the subject. [43] However, from 908 to 911

Muhammad ibn Abd al-Malik ibn Shabrit (al-Tawil), the Muladi operating in the Huesca-Lerida region, conducted attacks against Navarre and the western frontier of the Spanish March. In 912 Muhammad al-Tawil ravaged the Tarrega valley through which flows the Cervera River and in the following year died, probably while on a raid into the March. After his death relative quiet appears to have returned to the Catalan region.

Guifred II extended his dominion beyond the Llobregat River and subsequently Sunyer in 929 built a strong fortress as far south as Olérdola in the modern province of Barcelona, some three miles from Villafranca del Penedés. In the interim the western Christian kingdoms were in constant conflict with Moslems.[44]

In the absence of written historical evidence for the rather tranquil state of affairs between the Spanish March and Cordoba only conjectures can be offered for the period. The Cordoban emirate looked upon the western kingdoms as independent entities which posed a threat to the emirate's northern frontiers, particularly to Zaragoza, capital of the region, and to the areas surrounding Huesca and Lerida, all important cities and strongholds. However, the Moslems did not view the Catalan counties in a similar vein. They were also regarded as still part of the Carolingian body politic which, because of internal disintegration, were not considered dangerous to Cordoba's security.

It was against that background that Sunyer's family governed. He had two sons, Borrell and Miró. They succeeded their father and governed jointly until Miró's death in 966, after which Borrell was sole ruler; he died in 992. In 948 Borrell inherited from his uncle Sunifred II the county of Urgel. Hence, to his other three *honores* the latter was added. Upon his death he left the counties of Barcelona, Gerona, and Ausona to the eldest son, Ramón Borrell I (992-1018), and to the youngest, Ermengol, the county of Urgel.

Of the two brothers—Borrell (947-992) and Miró (947-966)—the first emerged as the preeminent of the two, not only because he outlived Miró by slightly more than a quarter of a century, but in the manner in which he weathered Al-Mansur's invasion of Catalonia. He exercised considerable initiative in the construction of irrigation facilities leading to the expansion of the region's agricultural base. When Miró died in 966, Borrell was left in sole control of the county of Barcelona. Borrell attempted without success to establish an ecclesiastical center independent of Narbonne, an effort started while Miró was still alive. This activity and strong support for monasteries and church development in his domains led Borrell to approach Rome personally. One consequence of his trip and initiatives to obtain papal support for church objectives was a gradual veering towards Rome and away from the French monarch.[45]

Arab issues were also of importance. In 863 Borrell and Miró had joined the King of Navarre and the Count of Castile against Al-Hakam, the first instance of a Catalan count of major importance aligning himself for a military action against Cordoba. The endeavor ended in disaster for the Christians, however. Consequently, Borrell sought renewal of the peace arrangement entered by his father with Al-Hakam many years before. Al-Hakam concurred but at a humiliating price. It was shortly after the agreement had been reached that Miró passed away.[46]

Borrell's great crisis occurred in 985 when Al-Mansur prepared a major expedition against Barcelona. Borrell attempted to block the Moslem entry into Catalonia by meeting the enemy forces beyond his borders, but failed in the attempt. The Islamic army, with a clear path to Barcelona and backed up by a Moslem fleet blocking the port, took and sacked the city. After occupying the city for some six months, the Moslems withdrew, taking with them as prisoners some of Barcelona's distinguished personalities.

Borrell retreated deeper into his territories to regroup for further defense while conducting diplomatic initiatives with Cordoba to purchase a badly needed peace. An appeal to the French monarch for help had gone unheeded, probably because of the latter's own internal problems. But Borrell's diplomacy with Cordoba led dangerously close to a state of vassalage. Nevertheless, for the remainder of his life he strove vigorously to rebuild Barcelona and the county's economy, and to restore destroyed monasteries. By the time of his death in 992, Borrell left his heirs in a position to better defend their inheritance when Al-Mansur's son once again led a punishing invasion in 1003, one year after his father's death. He probably launched the invasion in response to border adventures by Ramón Borrell (ruled 992-1018). The two were able to recover sufficiently from Abd al-

Malik's death in 1008. Without Borrell's energetic and astute diplomatic activities the recovery from the second assault would have been extremely difficult, if not impossible. Further, the lack of assistance requested of the French crown loosened the vassalage connection to the point that the House of Barcelona achieved true independence. That for generations onward documents referred to a French monarch was a matter of style and tradition rather than of substance.

Borrell left the counties of Barcelona, Gerona, and Ausona to Ramón Borrell I (at times referred to as Borrell III), the older of the two brothers. Ermengol inherited the county of Urgel. It should be noted again that Borrell II had received Urgel as an inheritance after the death of his uncle Sunifred II, Count of Urgel. It was fortunate for the future unity of Catalonia that the nucleus of Barcelona, Gerona, and Austona—originally the work of Guifred the Hairy—remained intact in the hands of one count. Ramón Borrell and Ermengol continued to work in harmony, coordinating their respective internal and external policies. When Ermengol died in 1010 during the Cordoban military campaign, Ramón Borrell retained the regency of Urgel and tutorship of Ermengol's son, Ermengol II. He discharged honorably obligations towards his nephew, but the responsibility gave him additional power and preeminence among the Catalan counts. The objectives of the two brothers, continued by Ramón Borrell, involved actions independent of the French crown, such as military intrusions into Cordoba's affairs and later into those of Zaragoza; territorial expansion and consolidation at the expense of the Moslems; intensified efforts at repopulation; strengthening the internal economy by encouraging monetization; and fostering close relations with the pope in Rome.

When Sulayman al-Mustayn (ruled 1012-1016) precariously held power in Cordoba, he confirmed for his supporter Mundhir ibn Yahya of the Tuchibi branch of the Arab Banu Hashim possession of Zaragoza. Given the disintegration of the caliphate, the measure in effect made Mundhir petty ruler of the domain. The Cordoban venture of the two counts led to close relations between Ramón Borrell and Mundhir. In fact, when Count Sancho García (ruled 995-1017) of Castile and Ramón Borrell decided on a dynastic alliance, stemming in part from the Catalan count's successful interference in Moslem affairs, the marriage arrangement took place during a meeting of the two counts in Zaragoza. Although Sancha, the Castilian count's daughter, and Ramón Borrell's son, Brenguer Ramón I (ruled 1018-1035), were children, the legal agreement eventually reached fruition. The dynastic linkage completed family interrelationships between the leading rulers of the Christian domains, contributing to a growing sense of common Christian interest in dealing with events in Andalusia.[47]

Ramón Borrell's expansion reachd the Segre and Ebro Rivers and his frontiers engulfed the basin of the Gaya River. However, he failed to develop a position from which he could plan on taking the city of Tarragona. Had he lived longer (he died at age 45) he may well have achieved that objective. It would have permitted him to restore Tarragona as the seat of a Catalan metropolitan, thus eliminating Narbonne's religious predominance over Catalan prelates. Earlier attempts to develop this independent role for Vich had failed. Ramón Borrell's support for the church was intense and associations with Catalan prelates close. When the expedition to Cordoba was decided, the bishops of Barcelona, Gerona, and Vich accompanied the military force. In the ensuing fighting the influential Arnulf, Bishop of Vich, and his colleague from Gerona were mortally wounded. Those were the days when bishops were as much warriors and politicians as ecclesiastics.

The Catalan House of Barcelona did not hesitate to extend grants and privileges to monasteries, churches, and prelates; but, sensitivity or penchant for legal sanction led members of this group to seek papal confirmation and assistance in serious confrontations among church leaders. In this way they differed from their Christian regal peers who were much less concerned about papal actions. An interesting development, which helped the evolution of closer relations with Rome, was the elevation in 999 of Pope Silvester II (Gerbert). He was a monk who had spent part of his youth in Vich and Ripoll in study and developed a position of considerable power in the imperial courts of Otto I and Otto II of Germany. Gerbert had acquired a widespread reputation as a teacher and scholar, particularly in mathematics and astronomy, skills acquired in Catalonia where he was highly esteemed. The extent of the two brothers' interest in securing papal support was reflected in two trips to Rome made by

Ermengol, and one by Ramón Borrell, where they experienced a warm reception and reasonable cooperation.[48]

Ramón Borrell died in 1018 and was succeeded by his son, a minor, Berenguer Ramón I. The count had married Ermesinda, daughter of Roger I, Count of Carcassonne, reputedly beautiful, talented, and strong-willed, who governed jointly with her son. When Berenguer Ramón reached majority age, the Countess Ermesinda was reluctant to give up her rule, a situation which led to stressful relations between the two. The issue was settled in 1023 when she pledged numerous properties and castles as bond for compliance in not thwarting her son's rule. Apparently, harmony reigned from then on.

Berenguer Ramón's period of rule was devoid of notable events. He attended carefully to the defense of the frontiers and resisted efforts of neighboring counts to interfere in his country, particularly those of Cerdanya, Besalu, and Ampurias. In 1035 he died; historical records shed little else about his reign.

Other Catalan Counties

The position of the Count of Barcelona, Ausona, and Gerona was one of preeminence with respect to the counts of other smaller counties in the region. Size of domains and the importance of Barcelona with its monetarized economy and trading relations throughout the Mediterranean, as well as warships, strengthened the House of Barcelona. Guifred's early wisdom in repopulating the rich plains in the Vich region were policies pursued further south beyond the Llobregat River by his successors, bolstering sharply the preponderance of the Barcelona counts.

Nevertheless, the absorption of the other counties took centuries as did also the development of a sense of Catalan consciousness. Bessalú passed to the counts of Barcelona in 1111, Cerdanya-Confluent in 1117. Lower Pallars went to Alfonso I, King of Aragon (1162-1196) and Count of Barcelona, of the same lineage. His son, Pedro II (ruled 1196-1212), through an agreement with Hugh III, Count of Ampúrias, incorporated that region into his domain. Jaime I, the Conqueror (ruled 1213-1276), received from Aurembaix, the childless Countess of Urgel, her ancient county. Upper Pallars was linked to the crown during Pedro II's reign.

The period ending about 1035 can be considered as a watershed in relations between Christian Spain and Andalusia. The reason for this view stems from the disintegration of the caliphate, the strength of the expanded central and western kingdoms, and entry of the Catalan counts, who were capable of taking advantage of the new situation to their south. My examination of early Catalan history supports the notion that approximately 1035 is an important historical divide for the Catalans as well.

Conclusions

To a large extent this account of the early development of Catalonia focused on dynastic diplomacy involving only political elites, many of them within the context of Carolingian political history. While this may appear to the casual reader as very old fashioned history, devoid of any discussion of peasants and cultural features, for example, or elegant theoretical constructs, the fact remains that Catalan political configurations and economic patterns of behavior were driven by the activities of key families and rulers across many centuries. Second, what is remarkable is the extent and widespread nature of the practice of familial politics that played out in the governments of counties and kingdoms, almost the same way families in business in the late twentieth century ran many of their own firms. Families in what today is Germany, southern France, and Italy, were involved directly in political affairs in what is modern-day Catalonia. Even popes participated, and we saw that one actually came from Catalonia. Third, the interactions among the Christians attempting to gain control over Catalan territory were even more complex than the story of Christian-Moslem relations on the borders of Catalonia.

It is precisely because of the consolidations of various political constructs in what is today Catalonia that it became possible for this area to begin the process of developing its own cultural, and not just political, identity. Repopulation activities, for example, did not happen by accident; they were fostered by kings and counts and grew out of strategic considerations.

Politics also influenced what areas might be depopulated. The tactics of these rulers in where to place monasteries and how to support various factions of the Church also influenced the development of local versus remote church-state relations.

Thus, increasingly when looking at the early origins of ethnic diversity of an Iberian region, there is much to be said about looking at the role of political elites in the process as opposed to the more recent approach of simply cataloging which peoples moved in and out of an area. At least in the case of Catalonia, ethnic identity was facilitated in large part by the activities of political families and ambitious rulers. For that reason, looking at the complex story of myriad rulers, while often tedious, becomes essential when examining the early history of Iberia. The same strategy is just as useful in looking at the early nation-building activities of such other Iberian regions as Navarre, Asturias, and, of course, Castile.

CHAPTER FIVE
CONSEQUENCES FOR CATALONIA:
SOME CONCLUDING THOUGHTS

Interest in regional European history has long existed among Europeans historians and local residents. However, with the resurgence of interest in regional and federated local governments across Europe during the last quarter of the twentieth century, has increased the necessity to understand what differentiates one area from another has also increased. This is as true for the seventeen legal regions of Spain as it is for northern Italy, and the key parts of the United Kingdom. In this respect, the Catalans are no different. However, Spaniards and historians alike have long realized that Catalonia was unique in many of its cultural, social, legal, and political ways from other parts of Spain. In some ways Catalonia's history must almost seem like a fable because during the Middle Ages it was a kingdom that extended all the way to Greece and was a mighty trading nation. In the mid-nineteenth century, Catalans entered a new era of self-recognition that has extended on and off to the present. All of those circumstances have led to renewed interest in the historical origins of this region.

The basic premise of this monograph has been to point out that long before the Middle Ages much was going in what is now Catalonia that sowed the seeds of local differentiation from the rest of Iberia. It is also a period in local history that has remained confused, improperly ordered, unapproachable, and often simply ignored. Hopefully, this small collection of essays will rectify some of that confusion.

To be sure, for centuries Castile and Catalans clashed for many reasons, but fundamentally there were sufficient differences between them to make their confrontations long a central theme in Spanish history, one that could not be ignored by any generation of historians and political and economic leaders. Unlike the Castilians, the Catalans had political and economic heritages that one could identify earlier as influencing significantly its character. These included the feudal experience, later the development of a middle class supported by trade, and then industrialization, and usually political subjugation to other political forces, such as to the Romans, the Carolingian Empire, Castile, and today Spain in general. These experiences in turn created earlier than elsewhere in Spain a distinct national (regional) identity. In large part this was made possible by the smallness of the area involved, which meant faster and more frequent communications than was possible in other parts of the peninsula that were less densely populated, far poorer, and covered wider spans of land. Because of Catalonia's juxtaposition between Iberia and France on the one hand and its proximity to the Mediterranean on the other, it acquired its own language, culture, legal traditions, and attitudes towards civic life and political institutions different from those of the Castilians. The traffic of invaders and immigrants who either sailed to Catalonia or walked into it from across the Pyrenees, or even up to it from central and southern Spain, also gave the area a heterogeneity that contrasted sharply to the culturally and politically more introspective and less varied societies of central or, for that matter, north-central Spain.

Early political differences could be traced to the feudal experiences of both. Catalonia clearly had become as feudal a society as any seen, for instance in southern France, particularly as one moved closer to the Pyrenaic frontier. Life became less feudal as one shifted southward and to the west until the borders with Islamic-controlled lands appeared, or, if one reached Christian central Spain. Thus, by the time one reached the Kingdom of Valencia, for example, feudalism was almost absent. While war was an important function in feudal Spanish society, and along the frontiers of all Iberian kingdoms, it had less of a pervasive influence on the political mindset of Catalans than upon other Iberians.

In central Spain it was more obvious that the Middle Ages had been a period during which there evolved a warlike culture where success was measured frequently by military results gained at the expense of neighboring kingdoms and later, in the unifying effort directed against Islamic kingdoms. A tough, warlike society always in danger, its borders constantly changing, and its fortunes tied to the expansion of control over new lands and towns, even in acquiring depopulated areas, led to a more limited political freedom of action for the nobility than found in Catalonia. Military necessity encouraged a more centralized form of administration leading to the development of the Kingdom of Castile with a strong monarch who, because of many generations' of successful military activity was, by the late 1400s, a very large kingdom and, therefore, could become the nucleus of the modern Spanish nation-state.

The process of political "homogenization" was consistent with what was happening elsewhere in Europe.[1] Castile, in effect, continued its successful expansion and gained control of Catalonia, indirectly at first through the famous marriage of Ferdinand and Isabel and later through military and political rule that, over subsequent centuries, led to the imposition of Castilian laws and control over the objections of the Catalans. Yet the process of cultural homogenization was imperfect, particularly during the period from 1700 to 1931, such that ethnic differences were not stamped out to the degree they were in other countries. The result was that Catalonia's culture and language survived, becoming the carrier of a list of regional aspirations that included at the very top autonomy from Castilian political control. Economic variations between life in Catalonia and Castile simply reinforced the differences between the two. Castile, overwhelmingly agricultural for centuries, stood in sharp contrast to the Catalans who also traded and then manufactured and always, because of their more urban concentration, offered services to a far greater extent than Castile, such as banking. Further proof of the yet incomplete homogenization was also apparent elsewhere in Iberia to a greater extent than seen in other parts of Europe; one has only to think in particular about the Basques.

While this not the place to describe in detail what happened between the Catalans and the Castilians from medieval times to the present, the point of differentiation has to be made. Simply note that over the past one thousand years the two groups were identifiable and felt that they had to "deal" with each other. That led to civil wars, invasions, proscriptions, and suppression of the Catalan language and culture. In Catalonia the feudal concept of vassalage to leadership evolved into the practices of contractual relations which in time provided patterns of economic and political behavior bonding together Catalans. That linkage was characterized by the Latinized language and its attendant cultural features, such as the arts and literature. Early on, therefore, the recognition that all Catalans had rights and privileges became a feature of that society in contrast to the Castilians who maintained a more militaristic approach to societal structure, because of the wars and threats of wars which exceeded those evident in northeastern Spain. The well-understood notion that the Catalans were far more legalistic than the Castilians, even obsessed with pactist or contractual law, emerged out of the different experiences of the Catalans.

In turn, that affected the nature of Catalan political practices. The most obvious example of this was the very early creation of a written constitution. The written *Usatges* (1058-1075) cataloged long standing Catalan customs as a very early example of such an approach to legal and political institutions. Nothing of that kind existed in Castile. Implicit and explicit in this document was the recognition that the middle class (burghers) had equality with the nobility, whereas in Castile the concept of vassalage to the king was more pronounced, because of the problem of war, but also since there were hardly any burghers to speak off who could ally with the nobles against the king; there simply only existed the landed nobility and agricultural peasants.

The idea of pactist law in Catalan affairs remained consistently present down to the modern era. One student of Catalan affairs made the obvious point: "What is remarkable is the measure of survival of contractualism, patrimonial or individualistic, in Catalan civil law through the ages, a law that even the Francoist dictatorship in the XXth century did not dare dismantle completely." [2] In the democracy that emerged subsequent to General Francisco Franco's regime, almost immediately the Catalans demanded and obtained further recognition of their legal and political "rights." They once again reactivated their own parliament and rekindled use of the Catalan language in legal, political, and educational activities.

The economic and social features of Castile were very different. Catalan burghers could align with nobles to insure their rights against kings but in Castile that whole class was mostly absent until modern times. The rights of individuals could not develop as fast and so the authoritarian features of an absolute monarchy were preserved and nurtured longer. Over the centuries central Spain paid less attention to the rights of individuals than in Catalonia, bumping directly against a growing pactist heritage in the northeastern corner of the peninsula. Add suppression of local culture by an expanding Castile and one has all the makings of a well-honed ethnic/regionalist problem that survived to the present. Given the fact that Catalonia is also not a small region, one could expect Catalan aspirations to thrive deep into the future.

In modern times the differences could still easily be identified. Catalan society, for instance, embraced republican politics faster and earlier than in Castile. During the civil war of 1936-39, Catalonia represented the most thorough republican/parliamentarian sector of Spain.[3] Elsewhere in the Republican zones, serious rifts existed between those who believed in political tolerance, constitutional law and authority, and rights of individuals while others, more in the majority, deeply subscribed to a more authoritarian tradition. As always, even in this war, the Basques operated largely apart, primarily because of their geographical separation from the rest of Republican Spain, but also with distinct differences of views. For example, Basques were more pro-Catholic while Republicans had generally and militantly become hostile to the Church.

In the period following Franco's death (since 1975), the Catalans reinstated their democratic approach to local government, exhibited a greater inclination to negotiate with Madrid for rights, but have also been adamant in asserting their distinctiveness from Castile. The central government had to bend more to the forces of federalist politics by acknowledging regionalist differences. The Catalans remain relatively prosperous when compared to the Castilians and determined to use all of their resources—particularly economic and intellectual—to state the case for Catalonia. Limited by economic difficulties, the real dangers presented by a militant Basque separatist movement for so many years, and the fragility of a new democratic monarchy in the late twentieth century in a land with long authoritarian experience, made it possible again for the Catalans to see themselves as different from Castile, continuing a pattern of behavior which threaded its way back deep into Iberian history.

Finally, we can ask, what influence has recent Islamic terrorist threats and attacks on Europe, and specifically in Spain, during the early years of the twenty-first century had on Catalonia? To be sure, angst over personal security and threats to national economic and political security are real. Will Madrid exert more military/police authority over many activities across all of Spain similar to those of the Francoist regime? What will happen to personal civil rights? Will terrorists attack Barcelona or other parts of Catalonia leading to closer bonds with Madrid? These are difficult questions to answer, but there to be dealt with within the framework of longstanding Catalan ways of living and governing.

ABOUT THE AUTHOR

James W. Cortada was trained in Spanish history at Florida State University, where he received an M.A. and Ph.D. in European history. He also studied at the University of Barcelona. Dr. Cortada is the author of nine books on Spanish history, most dealing with diplomatic history. He has published dozens of articles on Spanish history in such journals as *Iberian Studies*, *Cuadernos de Historia Economica de Cataluña*, *Renaissance and Reformation*, *Revista de Historia de America*, and the *Journal of Contemporary History*. He is a member of the Society for Spanish and Portuguese Historical Society and the American Historical Association. Dr. Cortada works at IBM Corporation.

He may be reached at 2917 Irvington Way, Madison, Wisconsin 53713 USA or at jwcorta@us.ibm.com.

END NOTES

[1]J.M. Monner Sans, *Dos monumentos druídos en Senterada* (Barcelona, 1872).
[2]Antonio de Forarull, *Historia crítica (civil y eclesiástical) de Cataluña* (Barcelona: Juan Aleu y Fugarull, 1876), 8 vols.
[3]Emile Cartilhac, *Les âges préhistoriques de l'Espagne et de Portugal* (Paris, 1886); Juan Vilanova Pierra and Juan de Dios de la Rada Delgado, *Geología y protohistoria ibéricas* (Madrid, 1890); Manuel Cazurro, *Las cuevas de Serrinilla y otras estaciones prehistóricas del n.e. de Cataluña* (Barcelona, 1908).
[4]José Manuel Gómez-Tabanera (ed.), *Las raices de España* (Barcelona, 1962).
[5]For details, see Miguel Tarradell Mateu, *Les Arrels de Catalunya* (1962).
[6] For example, *Colloqui internacional d'Arqueologia de Pirineus I veins al 3r milleniac. XII Colloqui international d'Arqueologia de Puigcerdà* (Puigcerdà: Institut d'Estudis Ceretans, 2003).
[7]For example, see Felipe Fernández-Armesto, *Civilizations: Culture, Ambition, and the Transformation of Nature* (New York: Free Press, 2001).
[8]Mateu, *Arrels de Catalunya* ; Michael Bouille and Claude Colomer, *Histoire des Catalans* (Toulouse : Editions Milan, 1990) :15-24.
[9]Luis Pericot García, *Historia de España* (Barcelona, 1934): 64-65.
[10]For details, see Martín Almagro Basch, *El covacho con pinturas rupestres de Cogul* (Lerida, 1952).
[11]Juan Maluquer de Motes, *Problemas de la prehistoria* (Barcelona, 1963): 25.
[12]A theme developed quite fully in Charles Redman, Steven James, Paul Fish, and J. Daniel Rogers (eds.), *The Archaeology of Global Change: The Impact of Humans on Their Environment* (Washington, D.C.: Smithsonian Books, 2004), one of many similar studies.
[13] The role of geography in creating civilizations has recently experienced a renaissance. Out of many possible examples, see Fernández-Armesto, *Civilizations*, 15-35.

[14]For details and background, see Julio Caro Baroja, *España primitive y romana* (Madrid, 1957); Martín Almagro Basch, *Orígen y formación del puebro híspano* (Barcelona, 1958); Luis Pericot García and Eduardo Ripoll Perellò (eds.), *Prehistoric Art of the Western Mediterranean and the Sahara* (Chicago, 1964); Antonio Arribas, *The Iberians* (New York, 1964).

[15]Fernández-Armesto, *Civilizations*, 347-378.

[16]Tarradell, Les Arrels de Catalunya, 84-90.

[17]Ibid., 96-7.

[18]For his views, see *La España primitive* (Barcelona, 1950) and especially his *Civilización megalítica catalana y la cultura pirenaica* (Barcelona, 1925) and revised and updated in his *Los sepulcros megalíticos catalanes y la cultura pirenaica* (Barcelona, 1950). On the general subject in English, see Glyn Daniel, *The Megalithic Builders of Western Europe* (London, 1958).

[19] As with many prehistoric stages, chronology and age are continuing sources of argument among specialists. The introduction of Carbon 14 calibration methods in dating in this field has caused major reevaluations of previously believed chronologies. For an early report on its success and progress, see Colin Renfrew, "Carbon 14 and the Prehistory of Europe," *Scientific American* 225, no. 4 (October 1971): 63-72 and his edited work, *The Explanation of Culture Change: Models in Prehistory* (London, 1974) and a more recent account Sheridan Bowman, *Interpreting the Past: Radiocarbon Dating* (Berkeley, Cal.: University of California Press, 1990).

[20]J. P. Mallory, "Beaker Culture", *Encyclopedia of Indo-European Culture* (Fitzroy Dearborn, 1997).

[21]Fernández-Armesto, *Civilizations*.

[22]This evidence is summarized in C.H.V.Sutherland, *The Romans in Spain 217 B.C.-A.D. 117* (London, 1939) and by F.J. Wiseman, *Roman Spain* (London, 1956), and most recently by J.S. Richardson, *Hispaniae: Spain and the Development of Roman Imperialism, 218-82 B.C.* (Cambrige University Press, 1986): 41-42, 112-113.

[23]Josef Msranjes de Marimòn, *Compendio histórico, resumen y descripción de la antiquísima ciudad de Empurias* (Barcelona, 1803; 2nd ed. 1968 with introduction by Eduardo Ripio Perellò).

[24]Richardson, *Hispaniae*.

[25]Martín Almagro Basch, "Inscripciones Ampuritanas," *Anales del Instituto de Estudios Gerundenses* 2 (1947): 174-208, vol. 3 (1948): 36-89.

Chapter Two

[1] J.M. Blazquez, "Hispania Desde el Año 138 al 235," *Hispania* 132 (1976): 36; but also see the whole article too, 5-87; Luis G. de

Valdeavellano, *Historia de España* (Madrid: Alianza Editorial, 1980), 2: 132-141.

[2]Fernando Riurỏ y F. Cufí, "Prspecciones arquelỏgicas en Rosas (Gerona)," *Anales del Instituto de Estudios Gerundenses* 15 (1961-1962): 203-224.

[3]Ferran Soldevila, *Historia de España* (Barcelona, 1952), 1: 45.

[4]Adolph Schulten, *Hispania* (Barcelona, 1920), *passim*.

[5]C.H.V. Sutherland, *The Romans in Spain, 217 B.C.-A.D. 117* (New York: Barnes and Noble, 1971): 70.

[6]Francis J. Wiseman, *Roman Spain* (London: Bell, 1956): 36-37.

[7]Ibid., 37.

[8]Antonio Ballessteros Beretta, *Historia de España u su influencia en la historia universal* (Barcelona: Salvat Editores, 1943):643.

[9]On transportation systems that built on Roman roads see David Ringrose, *Transportation and Economic Stagnation in Spain, 1750-1850* (Durham, N.C.: Duke University Press, 1969).

[10]The social and economic consequences for Spain are detailed by Karen Eva Carr, *Vandals to Visigoths: Rural Settlement Patterns in Early Medieval Spain* (Ann Arbor, Mich.: University of Michigan Press, 2002).

[11]Blazquez, "Hispania Desde el Año 138 al 235," 70-76.

[12]Salvador Minguijon Adrian, *Historia del derecho Español* (Barcelona: Editorial Labor, 1953): 39-40.

[13]José Rubia Barcia (ed.), *Americo Castro and the Meaning of Spanish Civilization* (Berkeley, Cal.: University of California Press, 1976), especially by Guillermo Aaya goubet, "The Evolution of Castro's Theories," 52; Salvador de Madariaga, *Spain* (London: Jonathan Cape, 1946): 20-24; Americo Castro, *The Spaniards*, Trans. By Willard F. King and Selma Margaretten (Berkeley, Cal.: University of California Press, 1977); Claudio Sanchez Albornoz, *España: un enigma histórico* 2 vols (Buenas Aires, 1956), however, I used an English translation, *Spain: An Historical Enigma* (Madrid: Fundaciỏn Universitaria Española, 1975), also in two volumes.

[14]Roger Collins, *Early Medieval Spain* (London: Macmillan, 1983): 1-11.

Chapter Three

[1]For examples see, E.A. Thompson, *The Goths in Spain* (Oxford: Oxford University Press, 1969): 132-133; Manuel Tuñon de Lara (ed.), *Historia de España*, vol. 2, *Romanismo y germanismo. El despertar de los pueblos hispanicos* by Juan José Sayas Abengochea and Luis A. Garcí Moreno (Barcelona: Editorial Labor, 1982): 252-253; Ballesteros, *Historia de España*, I, p. 842.

²Harold V. Livermore, *The Origins of Spain and Portugal* (London: George Allen & Unwin, 1971): 76.

³Luis Suarez Fernandez, *Manual de historia universal* (Madrid: Espasa-Calpe, 1958, 2, p. 301.

⁴Fernan Soldevila, *Historia de España* (Barcelona: Ediciones Ariel, 1972), 2, p. 86.

⁵Luis Bertrand, *The History of Spain* (London: Eyre and Spottiswoode, 1934): 5.

⁶Alan Watson, *The Evolution of Law* (Baltimore: Johns Hopkins University Press, 1985): 88-89.

Chapter Four

¹For introductions to the subject of early distinctions among the regions see Thomas F. Glick, *Islamic and Christian Spain in the Early Middle Ages* (Princeton, N.J.: Princeton University Press, 1979) and Claudio Sánchez-Albornoz, *La España cristiana de los siglos VII á XI* (Madrid: Espasa-Calpe, 1980): 1-60; and on the Catalan area, James N. Cortada and James W. Cortada, "Prehistoric Regionalism in the Iberian Peninsula: The Evidence for Catalonia," *Iberian Studies* 6, no. 2 (Autumn 1977): 77-82.

²For a general introduction to the subject, see Peter Sahlins, *Boundaries: The Making of France and Spain in the Pyrenees* (Berkeley, Cal.: University of California Press, 1988); Claudio Sánchez-Albornorz, *Spain, A Historical Enigma*, 2 vols (Madrid: Fundacíon Universitaria Española, 1975); Salvador de Madariaga, *Spain* (London: Jonathan Cape, 1946); Americo Castro, *The Spaniards* (Berkeley, Cal.: University of California Press, 1971.).

³That circumstance has spread more recently to other sectors as parliamentary democracy took hold in Spain following the demise of the Franco dictatorship in the last quarter of the twentieth century.

⁴Joaquin Nadal Farreras and Philippe Wolfs (eds.), *Histoire de la Catalogne* (Toulouse: Editions Privat, 1982):7-32; Victor Alba, *Catalonia, A Profile* (New York: Praeger, 1975): 3-11; Madariaga, *Spain*, 141-176; Ferran Soldevila, *Historia de Catalunya* (Barcelona: Editorial Alpha, 1935) vol. 3: 1-4; James S. Ameland, *Honored Citizens of Barcelona: Patrician Culture and Class Relations, 1490-1717* (Princeton, N.J.: Princeton University Press, 1986): 68-72; Pierre Bonnasie, *La Catalogne* (Toulouse: Publications de l'Universite de Toulouse-Le Mirall, 1975) vol. 1; an excellent introduction to the region is Robert Hughes, *Barcelona* (New York: Knopf, 1992).

[5]On Catalonia's early history, see Archibald R. Lewis, *Development of Southern French and Catalan Society, 718-1050* (Austin, Tex.: University of Texas Press, 1965) which is a most useful source; but see also Pierre Bonnassie, *La Catalogne de milieu du Xe à la fin de l'XIe siecle* 2 vols (Toulouse: Association des Publications, Universitè de Toulouse, 1975-1976), especially vol. 1; G. Feliu Montfort, "El condado de Barcelona de los siglos IX y X," *Cuadernos de historía económica de Cataluña* 7 (1972): 10-32; F. Valls-Taberner and Ferran Soldevila, *Historía de Cataluña* (Barcelona: C.S.I.C., 1955) vols 1 and 2; Ferran Soldevila, *Historía de Catalunya* (Barcelona: Editorial Alpha, 1935-1938) vols 1 and 2; Joaquim Nadal Farreras and Philippe Wolff, *Histoire de la Catalogne* (Toulouse: Editions Privat, 1982); Antoni Ferret, *Compendi D'História de Catalunya (segles IX-XVI)* (Barcelona: Editorial Brugera, 1967); José Balari Jovany, *Origenes Históricos de Cataluña* (Abadia de San Cugat del Valles: Instituto de Cultura Romanica, 1964) 2 vols; Prospero de Bofarull y Mascaro, *Los Condes de Barcelona vindicados* (Barcelona: Imprenta Juan Oliveres y Monmany, 1836) vols 1-2; Narciso Feliu de la Peña y Farrell, *Anales de Cataluña* (Barcelona: Imprenta Josep Llopis, 1709) vols 1-3; Fray Francisco Diego, *Historia de los Victoriosissimos antiguos condes de Barcelona* (Barcelona: Imprenta en Casa de Sebastian de Cormellas, 1603, reprinted Valencia: Artes Gráficas Soler, 1974); Antonio de Bofarull y Brocá, *Historía Crítica de Cataluña* (Barcelona: Editor Juan Aleu y Fugarull, 1876) vols 1-9; Ramòn D'Abadal, *Historia de Catalunya. Els primers comtes catalans* (Barcelona: Editorial Vicens Vives, 1980), vol. 1; Santiago Sobreques Vidal, *Historia de Catalunya. Els grans comtes de Barcelona* (Barcelona: Editorial Vicens Vives, 1980), vol. 2; Jerónimo Pujades, *Crónica universal del principado de Cataluña* (Barcelona: Imprenta José Torner, 1829) vols 1-8.

[6]Ramòn D'Abadal, *Dels visigots als catalans* 2 vols (Barcelona: Edicions 62, 1974): vol. 1: 244-246; Stuart C. Easton, *The Era Of Charlemagne: Frankish State and Society* (Princeton, N.J.: Van Nostrand, 1961); Pierre Riche, *The Carolingians: A Family Who Forged Europe* (Philadelphia, Penn.: University of Pennsylvania Press, 1993): 233-234, 246, 265.

[7]Arnold Hottinger, *Die Mauren: Arabische Kultur in Spanien* (Zurich: Wilhelm Fink Verlag, 1995, 2005): 31-49.

[8]Salvador Minguijon y Adrian, *Historía del Derecho Español* (Barcelona: Editorial Labor, 1953): 303.

[9]The term "Spanish March" refers to an area in northeast Spain. The definitive line of the Spanish March was established in 812 in agreement with the Arabs. It extended along the inland boundary of the Panades (Penedes) area between the Llobregat and Gaya river basis; Ferran Valls ix Taberner, *Marca Hispánica* (Barcelona: Promociones y

Publicaciones Universitaries, 1987); Ramón D'Abadal, "El Dominio Carolingio en la Marca Peninsular Hispánica, siglos IX y X," *Cuadernos de historía* 2 (1968): 34-49 and his "Nota sobre la locución 'Marca Hispánica," *Boletin de la Real Academic de Buenas Letras de Barcelona* 27 (1957-1958): 108. On the *Ordinario imperil* see Riche, *Carolingians*, 145-148.

[10]Eleanor Shipley Duckett, *Carolingian Portraits: A Study in the Ninth Century* (Ann Arbor, Mich.: University of Michigan Press, 1962): 20-57; Riche, *Carolingians*, 149-153.

[11]Riche, *Carolingians*, 157-159.

[12]Justo Pérez de Urbel and Ricardo del Arco Garay, *España cristiana, Comienzos de la Reconquista (711-1038)* (Madrid: Espasa-Calpe, 1982): 273-412.

[13]Lewis, *Development of Southern French and Catalan Society*, 99-100.

[14]Ramón d'Abadal i de Vinyals, *Els Primer comtes catalans* (Barcelona: Planeta, 1979): 161-179.

[15]Anwar G. Chejne, *Mulsim Spain: Its History and Culture* (Minneapolis, Minn.: University of Minnesota Press, 1974): 21.

[16]D'Abadal, *Primer comtes catalans*, 162.

[17]Lourent Theis, *L'heritage des Charles: De la mort de Charlemagne aux evirons de l'an mil* (Paris: Editions du Seuil, 1990) vol. 1 : 14-36.

[18]Victor Duruy, *History of France* (New York : Thomas Crower, 1889) : 86-88.

[19]See, for example, the account by Theis, *L'heritage des Charles*, vol. 1 : 80-81; Riche, *Carolingians*, 160-162.

[20]Theis, *L'heritage des Charles*, vol. 1 : 46.

[21]Perez de Urbel, *Los Comienzos*, 456-459.

[22]Ibid.

[23]Lewis, *Development of Southern French and Catalan Society*, 177, 277-278; Yitzhakh Baer, *History of the Jews in Christian Spain* 2 vols (Philadelphia, Penn.: The Jewish Publication Society of America, 1983).

[24]D'Abadal, *Primer comtes catalans*, 38-39.

[25]Theis, L'heritage des Charles, vol. 2 :58, 126, 156.

[26]For details see James W. Cortada, "Between Muslim and Christian Worlds: The Pyrenaic Counties in a Frontier Age, 809-1035," forthcoming.

[27]D'Abadal, *Primer comtes catalans*, 17-35.

[28]Lewis, *Development of Southern French and Catalan Society*, 104-113.

[29]Theis, *L'heritage des Charles*, vol. 2 : 109-113.

[30]Riche, *Carolingians*, 234.

[31]This surge in local authority, so important to the development of Catalonia, is discussed by Riche, *Carolingians*, 219-238.

[32]Theis, *L'heritage des Charles*, vol. 2 : 188-191.

[33]D'Abadal, *Primers comtes catalans*, 217-354.

[34]Ibid. is a good example ; but see also Sobreques Vidal, *Historia de Catalunya*, vols. 1 and 2; Julio Valdeón, José Salrach, and Javier Zabalo, *Historia de España, Fedualismo y consolidación de los pueblos hispánicos* (Barcelona: Editorial Labor, 1980).

[35]L. Barrau-Dihigo and R. Masso i Torrents (eds.), *Gesta Comitum Barcenonensium* (Barcelona: Institut d'Estudis Catalans, 1925).

[36]D'Abadal, *Primer comtes catalans*, 70.

[37]Ibid., 71, 77.

[38]Ibid., 71.

[39]Pérez de Urbel, *Comienza de la Reconquista*, 280ff; Cortada, "Between Muslim and Christian Worlds"; on populations, see Bernard R. Reilly, *The Medieval Spains* (Cambridge: Cambridge University Press, 1993): 90-91 and Christian Folch Iglesias, "El poblament al nord-est de Catalunya durant la transicío a l'edat mitjana (segles V-XI dC)," *Annals de l'Institut d'Estudis Gironins* 46 (2005): 37-65.

[40]D'Abadal, *Primer comtes catalans*, 101.

[41]Bonnasie, *La Catalogne*, vol. 1 : 118.

[42]Levi-Provençal, *España Musulmana* (Madrid : Espasa-Calpe, 1950) : 11. His fuller study was *Histoire de l'Espagne musulmane*, 3 vols (Paris : G.P. Maisonneuve, 1950-1953).

[43]D'Abadal, *Primers comtes catalans*, 217-354.

[44]Reilly, *Medieval Spains*, 83-87.

[45]Bonnasie, *La Catalogne de Mileu Du Xe à la Fin Du XIe siecle*, vol. 1 : 177-183 ; Urbel, *España cristiana*, 489, 511-522.

[46]Urbel, *España cristiana*, 482-486.

[47]Ibid., 491-492.

[48]For biographical data on Gerbert, see Abbé Lausser, *Gerbert: Étude historique sur le diexieme siècle* (Geneva : Slatkine-Megariotis, 1976, original edition published 1866) ; Florence Trystram, *Le Coq et La Louve: Gerbert et l'an Mille* (Paris : Flammarion, 1982).

Chapter Five

[1]Savador Giner, "The Social Structure of Catalonia," *Iberian Studies* 14, nos 1-2 (Spring-Autumn 1985): 45.

[2]Ibid., 46.

[3]Useful introduction are Manuel Cruells, *La societat catalana Durant la guerra civil* (Barcelona, 1978) and Ronald Fraser, *Blood of Spain* (New York: Pantheon, 1979).

www.ingramcontent.com/pod-product-compliance
Lightning Source LLC
Chambersburg PA
CBHW032017090426

42741CB00006B/634